CONFIDENTIALITY FOR MENTAL HEALTH PROFESSIONALS

A Guide to Ethical and Legal Principles

ANNEGRET KÄMPF • BERNADETTE McSHERRY

JAMES OGLOFF • ALAN ROTHSCHILD

www.
AUSTRALIANACADEMICPRESS
.com.au

First published in 2009 from a completed manuscript presented to
Australian Academic Press
32 Jeays Street
Bowen Hills Qld 4006
Australia
www.australianacademicpress.com.au

National Library of Australia Cataloguing-in-Publication data:

Title:	Confidentiality for mental health professionals : a guide to ethical and legal principles / Annegret Kämpf ... [et al.]
Edition:	1st ed.
ISBN:	9781921513428 (pbk.)
Notes:	Includes index. Bibliography.
Subjects:	Mental health personnel--Professional ethics--Australia. Mental health personnel--Legal status, laws, etc.--Australia.
Other Authors/Contributors:	Kämpf, Annegret.
Dewey Number: 174.2	

Cover design by Maria Biaggini.

Contents

Acknowledgments

....

This book is based on research funded by an Australian Research Council Discovery Project Grant. The authors would like to thank Tali Budlender and Kathleen Patterson for their invaluable assistance in editing and formatting this book and Sandra Pyke for compiling the Index and Tables of Cases and Legislation.

Introduction

For most individuals who work in the mental health sector, consulting with clients or patients is a central feature of their professional work. Those seeking mental health care often talk about very sensitive matters, such as personal experiences, behavioural patterns and interpersonal relationships. It is therefore unsurprising that, sooner or later, mental health professionals will need to consider whether they are ethically or legally obliged to disclose certain information to third parties.

There is often confusion as to whether mental health professionals are obliged to disclose confidential information and, if they are obliged to make a disclosure, what information they may have to disclose and to whom. This confusion may arise, for example, when a mental health professional has reason to believe that his or her client or patient is:

- living in a family situation that might escalate into violence;
- at risk of suicide;
- working in a high-stress environment where he or she is no longer sufficiently fit to work; or
- putting himself or herself or others at risk of harm.

Making a decision as to whether or not to disclose confidential information can be difficult. There is little written from the Australian perspective on confidentiality relating specifically to mental health settings, and the existing ethical and legal standards are complex and confusing (Kämpf & McSherry, 2006).

Legal writing frequently uses terminology that is unfamiliar to mental health professionals and focuses disproportionately on legal duties. This may create the impression that there is a clearly identifiable and strictly applicable duty to disclose when this is not necessarily the case. International articles or reports may also lead mental health professionals to believe that overseas laws apply in Australia, but again this may not be the case. While philosophical ideas are likely to provide some guidance, they need to be articulated in ways that relate to practice; otherwise mental health professionals who seek advice in philosophy are still left with the difficult task of transferring abstract ideas to specific circumstances. In contrast, professional advice can be short and prescriptive, sometimes lacking a comprehensive consideration of underlying ethical and legal considerations that are necessary to make a balanced decision. Codes of ethics may not provide sufficient guidance as they are typically focused on one group of professionals, their professional interests and reputation.

This book aims to advise mental health professionals as to how to handle confidential information in professional practice. It does not aim to provide a rigid approach to confidentiality in ethics and law. Rather, it focuses on the actual decision-making process concerning whether or not to disclose confidential information. The book aims to guide mental health professionals towards finding a solution that is ethically and legally sound and able to be recognised as such by external authorities. Thus, the focus rests on:

1. identifying the criteria to be considered when deciding whether to disclose confidential information, and
2. clarifying how to make a decision that complies with current ethical and legal obligations concerning confidentiality.

The Structure of this Book

Chapter 1 considers the importance of confidentiality. Understanding the many reasons why confidentiality is important is fundamental to comprehending the rationale behind ethical and legal requirements for disclosure.

Chapter 2 focuses on the ethical framework for confidentiality. It outlines the differences between ethics in general, ethical principles and professional ethics. It examines what an ethical decision is and how to make it.

Chapter 3 examines professional codes of ethics, what guidance they give on dealing with confidential information and how to approach them.

Chapter 4 introduces the legal framework for protecting confidentiality. It explains how, and to what degree, the law currently protects confidential information. In particular, it examines in what ways mental health professionals might be subject to civil law claims in the law of contracts, torts and equity.

Chapter 5 addresses the current state of the common law. It clarifies that the common law in Australia does not establish a duty to disclose confidential information, but rather focuses on identifying situations in which mental health professionals are permitted to disclose confidential information on a discretionary basis.

Chapter 6 outlines relevant statutory provisions.

Thus chapters 4 to 6 aim to guide mental health professionals as to what legal requirements exist and how to identify situations in which mental health professionals should seek legal advice.

Chapter 7 introduces practical scenarios that reflect crucial elements of contemporary ethics and the law. These scenarios employ a narrative form to summarise earlier approaches and they elaborate on what these approaches mean in daily practice.

Chapter 8 provides a short summary of some of the central considerations of the previous chapters and provides some 'quick guides', which can serve as a reference tool for mental health professionals in practice and training.

While chapters 2 to 5 serve to introduce the ethical and legal framework of decision-making as to whether to disclose confidential information, the scenarios of Chapter Seven in this book aim to improve clarity and confidence for mental health professionals in deciding whether confidential information ought to be disclosed. They introduce a framework that mental health professionals can use to develop their own strategy of decision-making when solving dilemmas. This framework is based on considerations of current ethical principles and the application of the law to typical circumstances in mental health care. It also includes methods of critical reflection of the protected interests at stake, alternative approaches and potential outcomes.

This book has been written predominantly with psychological and psychiatric practice in mind. However, it addresses many aspects of practice that are relevant to other professionals working in the mental health sector. It is also acknowledged that many characteristics vary depending on the individual circumstances of each case and the nature of the therapeutic relationship.

CHAPTER 1

The Concept of Confidentiality

Confidentiality is a concept in ethics and law that protects the trust a person places in having private information kept secret. It stems from the premise that information imparted in certain circumstances among a limited number of persons gives rise to an obligation not to disclose that information to third parties.

The trust that information will not be divulged can stem from personal agreement or a general expectation. A mental health professional can reach a personal agreement on confidentiality with his or her client or patient, when he or she discusses in what circumstances and to what extent confidential information will be kept secret. This provides some clarity for both parties. The general expectation that private information will not be disclosed to others is more complicated, and it lies at the heart of the discussion concerning professional standards of confidentiality. By nature of the relationship, a client or patient typically expects confidentiality in therapeutic relationships. Whether, and to what degree, this expectation is realistic is controversial and varies in different cultures and individual settings, but a basic expectation exists.

It is important to note that the concept of confidentiality is linked to, and may be easily confused with, the legal concepts of privacy and privilege. Privacy is broader in scope than the concept of confidentiality. While privacy relates to the ownership of information and includes matters of collecting, storing and controlling information, confidentiality focuses on an individual's expectation that private information that was communicated to a limited number of persons will not be communicated to others. In this way, confidentiality is relational, while privacy reaches beyond the relationship between the confider and the person who receives the confidential information. The concept of privilege, however, is narrower than confidentiality. It applies to disclosure of confidential information in judicial settings only.

Why Confidentiality Needs Protection

When assessing whether or not to disclose confidential information, it is important to understand why confidentiality is protected in both ethics and law. This understanding helps to assess the demands of ethical and legal provisions, particularly where ethical and legal principles leave scope for interpretation by including formulations such as 'where reasonable', 'where necessary' or 'where appropriate'. It may also help to identify situations in which confidential information might have to be disclosed.

Both law and ethics have recognised the need to protect confidentiality for a variety of reasons. The basic premise as to why confidentiality has a fundamental standing in therapeutic care is that the therapeutic relationship includes many aspects of power imbalance, vulnerability and trust.

Clients or patients who consult with mental health professionals reveal sensitive information and place trust in these individuals to help them overcome their problems. In order to analyse or diagnose clients or patients correctly, an atmosphere of frank consultation must be established, enabling the problem's cause and impact to be understood. If clients or patients fear that the information will be disclosed to third parties, trust may be impaired.

Confidentiality in therapeutic settings is also important for many other reasons, ranging from clients' or patients' personal interests in maintaining confidentiality to professional and public interests. The following sections outline the main reasons why confidentiality is important. Although the reasons are categorised into personal, professional and public interests, many aspects interrelate. Outlining the reasons in this manner highlights the many levels that need to be kept in mind in order to understand confidentiality in therapeutic relationships.

Personal Interests
Facilitating Treatment
The promise of maintaining confidentiality is an important factor in encouraging persons who have mental health problems to seek treatment. It makes them feel safe when consulting mental health professionals about personal matters that they might not want to share with other persons. Given that the consultation with the client or patient is crucial in mental health care for diagnosis and treatment, trust is essential for facilitating the treatment of the client or patient.

Keeping Sensitive Information Private
Maintaining confidentiality in therapeutic settings is also important for the control of personal information. The information that clients or patients reveal to mental health professionals in the expectation that they will receive care and treatment for their mental health problems can be highly sensitive. Personal issues, such as anxieties, sexual relationships and histories of violence or drug abuse may be discussed. If this kind of information is raised in a context outside of the therapeutic setting, it can be misunderstood and misused. Therefore, it should be kept private or restricted to use within the therapeutic relationship.

Avoiding Stigmatisation and Discrimination
The simple fact that an individual receives mental health care can lead to stigmatisation and discrimination as mental illnesses and mental disorders are still subject to wide-ranging prejudices in society. Confidentiality in mental health services avoids information leaking into the community that a client or patient might find embarrassing, thus decreasing the chance that a person with a mental illness or mental disorder will be subject to stigmatisation and discrimination.

Safeguarding Certain Positions in Life
Individuals who are subject to stigmatisation and discrimination may lose, or not be able to access, certain positions or services in life. These may include, for example, employment and leadership positions and access to accommodation, health and life insurance.

Maintaining confidential mental health services decreases the likelihood of such negative outcomes.

Increasing Positive Ethical Outcomes

Maintaining confidentiality is linked to important moral principles, such as respect for autonomy, non-maleficence, beneficence and justice. Apart from this principle-based approach, other philosophical viewpoints value confidentiality as a virtue in itself, as a means to achieving individual treatment or improving public welfare, or as a core element of care in interpersonal relationships. Also, professional codes of ethics include the general principle that confidentiality should be protected. Thus, there are a variety of reasons why a mental health professional as well as a client or patient might value confidential therapy as an ethical practice.

Increasing Positive Health Outcomes for Other Individuals

Clients or patients who frankly discuss sensitive issues related to their mental health problems without fear of disclosure of information to third parties assist the mental health professional to diagnose the underlying issue, thereby advancing their proper treatment. Successful mental health care also improves the wellbeing of others such as family members, friends and colleagues who can be affected by an individual's mental illness or mental disorder.

Professional Interests

Facilitating Care and Good Practice

Health care is rooted in compassionate care and many mental health professionals are personally interested in the wellbeing of their clients and patients. These professionals genuinely want to serve their clients' or patients' interests through the provision of confidential health services.

Respecting Personal Morality

Maintaining confidentiality is also important to the personal morality and integrity of many mental health professionals. The decision to maintain confidentiality is closely associated to the personal ethics of the individual professional who may have a strong moral standing for keeping a promise or an expectation of confidentiality.

Corroborating Professional Reputation

Beyond the personal interests of the mental health professional in a successful practice, effective care and treatment reflect positively on the performance of his or her profession.

Public Interests

Strengthening Public Health and Welfare

Public health and welfare can be improved through effective mental health care, and mental health services that protect confidentiality increase public trust in these services. If a guarantee of confidentiality cannot be assumed, this may deter people from seeking professional help.

Protecting Confidentiality as a Human Right

Confidentiality has been increasingly acknowledged as a human rights issue, as the protection of confidentiality ties in with the protection of an individual's autonomy, self-determination and privacy. A standard of protection for confidentiality in mental health settings that is lower than the standard in general health settings may interfere with rights to equal treatment and non-discrimination.

Conclusion

These numerous justifications for protecting confidentiality indicate that mental health professionals must begin any decision-making process with the presumption that confidentiality is of fundamental importance. There are, however, exceptions to this basic idea. The following chapters explore some of those exceptions from both ethical and legal perspectives.

Key Points

- Confidentiality protects the trust a person places in another to not disclose personal information to third parties.
- The concept of privacy is broader in scope than that of confidentiality and relates to the ownership of information.
- The concept of privilege is narrower in scope than that of confidentiality and applies to disclosure of confidential information in judicial settings only.

- Mental health professionals should be aware that their decision to disclose confidential information can have consequences on different levels: on the individual client or patient, on themselves both personally and professionally, on their profession and on public interests.

- There are many reasons why confidentiality is important. Some, but not all, of these reasons can be explained on legal or ethical grounds.

- Legal and ethical principles alone may sometimes lack sufficient guidance for decision-making as they typically focus on some of these reasons only.

- This book focuses on the actual decision-making process as to whether or not to disclose confidential information, and on identifying the essential criteria that must be considered for the decision to be an appropriate one.

- It is important to start any decision-making process with the presumption that confidentiality should be protected.

Points of Reflection

- Familiarise yourself with the many reasons why confidentiality in mental health care is important.

- Consider why confidentiality is important for you, your client or patient, your profession and other people in society.

CHAPTER 2

The Ethical Framework
for Confidentiality

This chapter outlines the ethical background that underpins an analysis of whether or not to disclose confidential information in therapeutic settings. It explains what is meant by the term 'ethics' and what characterises the ethics of confidentiality in relation to mental health care. The chapter then introduces some of the most established theories of ethics and explores how they translate into practice.

The Meaning of Ethics

In a professional context, the term 'ethics' sometimes connotes formal rules and disciplinary action, but ethics is most commonly understood to be a branch of moral philosophy. The study of ethics is concerned with an understanding of human behaviour. It considers whether a course of action can be deemed right or wrong and for what reasons. In other words, the study of ethics aims to understand the following:

- whether there are universal moral claims, values or principles in human behaviour
- what ethics means in general (meta-ethics) or specific contexts (applied ethics)
- whether ethics can constitute a framework to guide moral behaviour (normative ethics).

Ian Kerridge, Michael Lowe and Cameron Stewart (2009, p. 1) describe ethics in the following terms: being concerned with human flourishing and wellbeing, prescribing what we *should* do rather than what we actually do, being universalisable in its relevance to

11

all individuals regardless of their religion, culture or other background, and following a systematic approach to recognising and defining what ought or ought not be done. They also state that ethics is often considered of such overriding importance that it is of greater significance than the law, politics or self-interests (p. 2). Although some of these elements may be disputed, they do provide a basic outline of the nature of ethics.

Peter Singer (1993, p. 10) points out that ethics has always been about motivations that reach beyond personal interests. His view is that being ethical involves putting oneself in the position of another, taking a universal point of view and deriving reason from basic ethical principles (p. 12). Yet, although ethics builds on universal ideas, determining what is right and wrong is likely to depend on the context in which the ethical question arises. The meaning of ethics may alter when it is applied to individual circumstances.

When the question of whether or not to disclose confidential information arises, ethics looks at the reasons why confidentiality in therapeutic settings is valued in general terms and why it is important in individual circumstances. An ethical perspective considers what it means to respect confidentiality in light of ethical values and reasoning, and it also identifies the conflicting interests that are at stake. When conflicts of interest arise, ethics aims to provide guidance on how to weigh such conflicting interests, but the considerations put forward by different ethical theories may lead to different results.

What Characterises the Ethics of Confidentiality in Mental Health Care?

When dealing with confidential information in therapeutic settings, two questions arise: First, in what ways do ethical theories clarify how to deal with confidential information? And second, are there any special issues to be taken into account when dealing with confidential information in the context of mental health care?

Chapter 1 dealt with some of the reasons why confidentiality in mental health care is important. In general, ethical theories concerning confidentiality examine the moral values related to maintaining and disclosing confidential information. These values may help provide a conceptual framework for decision-making in this area.

An understanding of ethics is important in general in our society, but the ethical value of confidentiality is of particular importance to health care professionals (see, e.g., Michalowski, 2003, p. 16ff). In this regard, it is important to consider the specific demands of the mental health professions. Ethical dilemmas in psychology are common. Psychology involves thoroughly engaging with the client to evaluate the client's health and to provide therapy and guidance, in particular through counselling. Ronald Francis characterises psychologists as being 'in the business of behaviour change' (1999, p. 81) in order to assist clients to improve their mental health and to help them become more self-determining and autonomous people. Thus, open and frank communication and trust in the therapeutic relationship is central to psychological practice.

In the context of psychiatry, Jennifer Radden (2002, p. 53) claims that the uniqueness of psychiatry calls for unique ethics. She argues that psychiatry's uniqueness stems from three features: the nature of the therapeutic relationship, the character of the patient and the therapeutic 'project'. Radden describes the therapeutic relationship as a 'key ingredient in therapeutic effectiveness' (p. 53) and considers it a 'treatment tool, analogous to the surgeon's scalpel' (p. 53). When considering the nature of the relationship, the special character of the patient plays an important role. Radden describes the character of the patient as showing 'vulnerability to exploitation, dependence and inherent inequality' (p. 53), in particular because of 'patients' diminished judgement, the stigma and controversy associated with their condition, and the salient place of gender in psychiatry' (p. 53). The therapeutic project aims to at least 'restore some earlier level of functioning and to relieve debilitating signs and symptoms' (p. 54) and at most will succeed in 're-forming the patient's whole self or character, when these terms are understood in holistic terms as the set of a person's long-term dispositions, capabilities and social and relational attributes (p. 54).

Radden's call for a specific ethics for psychiatry has been criticised (Crowden, 2003), and it may indeed be possible to apply existing methods of ethical thought to the context of psychiatry without creating a unique set of ethics for this profession. However, her assessment of the features of psychiatric care is revealing. She identifies the central and extraordinary importance of the therapeutic relationship in psychiatric care, and the complex ways in which it interrelates with the character of the patient, in particular his or her vulnerabilities and wellbeing, and with the patient's treatment as the therapeutic 'project'. Radden's approach also provides a starting point for assessing the special characteristics of other mental health professions: though the therapeutic project varies within different areas of mental health care, the therapeutic relationship and the special characteristics of the client or patient will have a similar standing in other mental health areas. In forensic settings, the psychiatrist's role of 'serving two masters' (Gutheil, 2009, p. 436), the patient and the legal system impedes on the level of trust within the relationship between the forensic psychiatrist and the patient, but does not negate that the premise that Radden describes still exists.

Thus, when considering whether to breach confidentiality in mental health settings, it is important to assess in what ways disclosing confidential information influences the therapeutic relationship, the mentally unwell client or patient, and his or her treatment.

Key Points

- Ethics is a branch of philosophy that analyses what is morally right or morally wrong human behaviour.
- Ethics approaches the question of what should be done as morally right or morally wrong behaviour based on generally relevant ideas, and it tries to systematically provide reasoned approaches based on ethical claims, values or principles.
- Many aspects of what is morally right and morally wrong behaviour depend on the context of the situation.
- When deciding what is morally right or morally wrong behaviour in mental health care, it is important to consider what is special about mental health care in comparison to other branches of health care. For example, differences may be found in the character of the relationship to the client or patient; the scope of practice; and the character, wellbeing and vulnerabilities of the client or patient.
- When the question arises as to whether confidential information may be disclosed, it is useful to reflect on what these considerations mean in relation to your own practice, your client or patient, and you personally.

Points of Reflection

- Identify the reasons why confidentiality is particularly important in mental health care and in relation to your own practice. What are your preferences and experiences?

- Consider how disclosing certain confidential information may affect the therapeutic relationship with your client or patient.

Ethical Theories

Psychologists who have a clear sense of what they believe and why they believe it are more likely to make good ethical decisions (Knapp & VandeCreek, 2006, p. 16). What then are the different theories of ethics? Len Sperry (2007, p. 472) describes an ethical theory as a perspective on an ethical situation that considers underlying values and provides a means of determining which values take priority in any given situation. This section provides a brief overview of the different positions in the study of ethics, focusing on a selection of the most influential theories of ethics (for further details see Beauchamp, 2009, p. 25ff). It will not assess which theory of ethics is the best one to follow. Rather, this chapter aims to explain the reasoning processes explored in theories of ethics. The understanding of these reasoning processes will later serve as a key feature for guiding mental health professionals as to what criteria to consider before deciding whether or not to disclose confidential information.

Consequentialism and Deontology

Two influential ethical theories are consequentialism and deontology. These theories display two fundamentally different views when deciding whether a course of action is morally right or wrong.

Consequentialism values a course of action depending on its potential outcome. According to consequentialist theory, a course of action is morally right if it produces the best consequences. The nature of the action or its motivation is not crucial for judging whether the action is right or wrong. Philosophers have developed many fine nuances within consequentialist theory. In the understanding of utilitarianism, a well-known form of consequentialist theory, the best consequences are the ones that lead to the greatest good for the greatest number of people (Bentham, 1793, p. 310). In classical theory, this maximisation of utility has been measured in happiness (Bentham, 1793, p. 310) or pleasure (Mill, 1895). But defining the greatest good can also be measured in other terms (Häyry, 2007, p. 58), such as quality of life (Moore & Baldwin, 1993, p. 61) or justice (Singer, 1993).

Many justifications as to why confidentiality is important follow consequentialist ideas. One process of reasoning is that if confidentiality is not systematically protected in therapeutic relationships, a client or patient might be deterred from services, or be less candid during consultations (Kottow, 1986). Therefore, it is also in the public interest to preserve confidentiality, 'to ensure that members of the public make effective use of professional services' (Milne, 1995, p. 170). Raanan Gillon (1986, p. 46) writes:

> The commonest justification for the duty of medical confidentiality is undoubtedly consequentialist: people's better health, welfare, the general good, and overall happiness are more likely to be attained if doctors are fully informed by their patients, and this is more likely if doctors undertake not to disclose their patients' secrets.

However, there is also the consequentialist argument that, particularly in mental health care settings, professionals should be permitted to disclose confidential information for reasons of public interest, such as if the disclosure serves to prevent danger to others and to enhance public safety. Thus, the consequentialist approach to determining whether an action is right or wrong is problematic when there are competing public interests at stake. The focus on the greatest number of people can lead to an automatic preference for public over individual interests. It is possible to safeguard individual interests as a matter of societal gain, but consequentialism may accept morally concerning actions such as torture or even killing, if it leads to a better outcome.

Another shortcoming of consequentialism is that it is hard to define 'good outcomes' in clear and undisputed terms and it may be difficult to predict these outcomes in advance. Is it good to detain a client or patient because he or she said that he or she might hurt someone? Is it good to let him or her go? On a more conceptual ground, is the prevention of potential bodily harm better than certain physical or medical restraint of the client or patient who uttered the threat? Can these questions be answered when looking only at consequences, or should motivations or other circumstances be considered as well?

In contrast to consequentialism, deontology looks at the nature of the action itself and considers whether a course of action is intrinsically right or wrong. Deontology stems from a belief that some rules in society can be regarded as inviolable in any circumstances, for example, a rule that no-one shall be subjected to torture as its use is always morally wrong. According to the duty-focused view of deontology, there is a moral obligation to restrain from taking intrinsically wrong actions.

In relation to confidentiality, the deontological position gives rise to a general moral duty to avoid passing on someone's remarks said in confidence, whether the recipient of the information is a friend, relative or colleague at work.

While consequentialism allows for methods of balancing conflicting interests, strict deontologists are limited in relation to what to do when conflicting duties are both intrinsically right or both intrinsically wrong. For example, if the question arises whether or not to disclose confidential information, deontologists have to consider the conflicting duties of the intrinsically right action of maintaining clients' or patients' confidentiality and the intrinsically right action of protecting persons from preventable harm or danger. However, Ian Kerridge, Michael Lowe and Cameron Stewart (2009, pp. 14–15) write: '[I]t appears that consequentialism is susceptible to many of the same criticisms as deontological theories because it is no easier to rank consequences than it is to rank moral rules'.

In the end, consequentialists and deontologists both defend confidentiality in therapeutic settings as a morally desirable goal. They just base their reasons on fundamentally different grounds.

Both positions can be modified to address some of their shortcomings, but both theories have also been subject to criticism and their use in practice is limited. Nevertheless, no matter how far these theories stand up to the demands of practice, they show how important it is to look at values from a different point of view. One of the obstacles to making a sound decision is to rely solely on one's intuition. Even though intuition can be a good guide for decision-making, it is important to question one's approach, and to provide reasons for one's position. Graham Davidson (1995, p. 156) writes in this regard:

> [W]here the confidentiality rule is challenged, [psychologists need] to be able to: analyse their own set of values that may affect such a decision; identify the ethical system in which they are operating and contrast it with alternative systems; and argue for their chosen line of action, taking into account ethical, professional and legal issues.

Virtue Ethics

Virtue ethics is another important ethical theory. Ian Kerridge, Michael Lowe and Cameron Stewart (2009, p. 16) state that '[v]irtue ethics contains the notion that the rightness or wrongness of an action is derived from the underlying motive of the person making that action'. According to virtue theory, a virtuous person acts according to moral motives. The theory emphasises the importance of 'character traits that promote virtuous behaviour' (Bloch & Green, 2006, p. 9). The classical virtues, which derive from the philosophy of Aristotle, include magnanimity, agreeableness, friendship, scientific knowledge, prudence, technical skill and wisdom (Bloch & Green, 2006, p. 9), with practical wisdom (phronesis) being the most important virtue for Aristotle (Crowden, 2003, p. 146).

In contemporary philosophy, the key virtues have been reassessed in light of modern demands and some philosophers concentrate their theory on a selection of some virtues only (Oakley & Cocking, 2001, p. 7). Jennifer Radden (2002, p. 55) considers that the virtues of medical practice extend to trustworthiness, honesty, kindness, humility, patience, compassion, phronesis, justice, fortitude, temperance, integrity and self-effacement. She states that the virtues in mental health care settings are marked by some additional features, including respect for confidentiality, fidelity, veracity and prudence, warmth and sensitivity, humility and perseverance (p. 55). However, Radden considers that not all of these elements may be virtues; in particular, she states that warmth may not be a virtue (p. 55).

Apart from problems with defining what constitutes a virtue, virtue theory runs the risk of circularity in argument. As Edmund Pellegrino and David Thomasma have pointed out: 'The right and good is that which the virtuous person would do and the virtuous person is one who would do right and good' (1993, p. 152). The theory of virtue ethics does not sufficiently explain why a course of action is right or wrong. Teaching virtues is therefore hard to achieve.

The Principle-Based Approach

In modern moral philosophy, Tom Beauchamp and James Childress (2001) have established a principle-based approach to ethical theory that combines aspects of deontological and utilitarian theories. They originally started with a theory of ethics that was based on 'four clusters of principles [that] derive from both considered judgments in the common morality and enduring and valuable parts of traditions of health care' (Beauchamp, 2007, p. 9). The common morality that they refer to has 10 elements and is 'applicable to all persons in all places, and all human conduct is rightly judged by its standards' (Beauchamp, 2007, p. 7). The 10 elements are that human beings shall (Beauchamp, 2007, p. 9):

1. not kill
2. not cause pain or suffering to others
3. prevent evil or harm from occurring
4. rescue persons in danger
5. tell the truth
6. nurture the young and dependent
7. keep promises
8. not steal
9. not punish the innocent; and
10. treat all persons with equal moral consideration.

These elements of common interest, according to Tom Beauchamp (2007, p. 7), 'have proven over time that their observation is essential to realise the objectives of morality. What justifies them is that they achieve the objectives of morality, not the fact that they are universally shared across cultures.'

Tom Beauchamp and James Childress then established four basic principles that 'incorporate and articulate the most general values of common morality' (Beauchamp, 2007, p. 7). These include (Beauchamp, 2007, p. 4):

1. non-maleficence — a principle requiring not causing harm to others;
2. beneficence — a principle requiring doing good to others through providing benefits and balancing benefits against risks and costs;
3. respect for autonomy — a principle requiring respect for the decision-making capacities of persons, their right to self-determination and freedom from control of others; and
4. justice — a principle requiring fair distribution of benefits, risks and costs and respecting the equality of all human beings.

These principles are categorised as giving rise to duties. This means that there is always a duty to follow the relevant principle unless it is in conflict with another duty (Beauchamp, 2007, p. 7). Indeed, the principles are not absolute, but rather allow for exceptions and are subject to modification and reformulation (Beauchamp, 2007, p. 8). If there is a conflict between principles, they need to be weighed and 'discretionary judgement becomes an inescapable part of moral thinking that relies on principles' (Beauchamp, 2007, p. 8). However, departure from the basic principles requires a consistent approach. Tom Beauchamp (2007, p. 8) and David DeGrazia (2003, p. 221ff) identify the following criteria for developing a consistent, principle-based set of beliefs:

1. consistency — decisions must avoid contradictions;
2. argumentative support — decisions must be explicitly supported with reasons;
3. intuitive plausibility — decisions must be credible when first made and upon reflection;
4. compatibility or coherence with reasonable non-moral beliefs — decisions must be consistent with empirical evidence, if it is available;
5. comprehensiveness — decisions must aim to cover the entire moral domain or as much of it as possible; and

6. simplicity — decisions must reduce the number of moral considerations to the minimum possible without sacrificing other criteria.

The principle-based approach has mainly been criticised on methodological grounds (Bloch & Green, 2006, p. 9). However, it has pragmatic features and provides a thorough tool for assessing how to make an ethical decision. In short, the principle-based approach identifies the underlying principles that deem an action to be right while also specifying what the result of that action would be in the specific circumstances. The approach then re-assesses on coherent grounds whether the action is still deemed right in that particular context.

....

Ethical Principles in Mental Health Care

Gerald Koocher and Patricia Keith-Spiegel (2008, p. 3) adopt the principle-based approach and combine it with ideas based on other classical theories of ethics. They identify the following core ethical principles for those working in the mental health field. Mental health professionals should:

- not harm the client or patient (non-maleficence) — they should act to eliminate or minimise any potential for damage;
- respect the autonomy of the client or patient and work with him or her towards greater self-reliance and self-determination;
- be just to the client or patient and to treat him or her fairly and equitably;
- be faithful, loyal and truthful with the client or patient to allow him or her to feel as safe and free as possible;
- accord the dignity of each client or patient and view him or her as worthy of respect despite existing differences;
- treat the client or patient with care and compassion;
- pursue excellence in delivering quality mental health services;
- be accountable for errors and their consequences, and accept responsibility; and
- be courageous in actively upholding ethical principles.

Key Points

- There is a range of fundamentally different theories of ethics that consider outcomes or actions as morally right or morally wrong. The most established theories in medical ethics all value the maintenance of confidentiality in therapeutic settings.

- In ethical theory, there are a variety of justifications for maintaining confidentiality in therapeutic relationships. These justifications include attempting to provide:

  - that the action is providing the best outcomes for individuals or for public health;
  - that the action is an intrinsically right action in itself;
  - that the action is one performed by a virtuous person; and
  - that the action is right according to specific moral principles.

Points of Reflection

- Reflect on the different ethical approaches outlined to identify why confidentiality in mental health care is important.

- Consider in what ways the reasoning of the different ethical approaches derives from respecting certain values, and identify which values are important to you, your client or patient and your profession.

- Learn to identify the reasons for your actions. Contemplate whether they are motivated by personal intuition or by a set of general values and in what ways they might be modified in specific circumstances.

- Once you have considered your ethical approach and the reasons why you follow it, reconsider this approach in relation to various examples. These examples may be hypothetical or may arise from your training or practice. Ask yourself what you would do and why? And, how does this fit into your system of decision-making?

CHAPTER 3

Codes of Ethics

....

This chapter examines the rules of relevant codes of ethics that relate to confidentiality. It first examines why codes of ethics may provide a useful starting point for guidance in decision-making about whether or not to disclose confidential information. It then analyses the rules dealing with confidentiality in the relevant codes of ethics.

While ethical approaches start with an internal assessment of how to behave (Kerridge et al., 2009, p. 1), codes of ethics consist of rules defined by an outside body. Mental health practice has long been concerned with ethical dilemmas arising from human behaviour, but codified ethics in the mental health profession is a recent phenomenon (Bloch & Pargiter, 2009, p. 151ff).

The understanding of how to address, or react to, ethical dilemmas in mental health practice can be seen as a matter of moral philosophy being applied to given circumstances. Applying ethical theories to practice requires identification of fundamental moral principles, considering them in context and weighing them in the light of other, possibly conflicting, moral principles. However, practitioners who are faced with an ethical dilemma may not find moral philosophy immediately helpful to their concerns, as it requires a sophisticated understanding of different ethical theories and professional training concerning what they mean in practice.

Codes of ethics are more readily available and easier to understand. They draw upon moral philosophy, incorporating this into practical guidelines and defining the ethical standards of the profession. Typically, they focus on the most common issues for the profession and express the current position of a relevant professional body on how to approach matters of concern. Thus, codes of ethics can be viewed as a collection of ideas that best translate into the practice of the profession. Many codes of ethics have adopted the ideas of principle-based ethics — probably because this approach translates well into practice and can be quite easily understood. However, the formulation of codes of ethics must balance theory and practice. While codes of ethics aim to outline the underlying moral principles that need to be considered, they also need to be sufficiently precise about how professionals should act in practice. At the same time, if codes of ethics are too precise, they run the risk of being overly long, complicated and subject to detailed interpretation that may be detached from the underlying moral principles.

Beyond providing direct guidance to professionals on what to consider in given circumstances, codes of ethics serve other purposes. In relation to psychiatry, Sidney Bloch and Russell Pargiter (2009, p. 156) identify four principal purposes for codes of ethics:

- to protect and promote the professional status of psychiatrists
- to serve as an intrinsic part of a process of self-regulation
- to sensitise psychiatrists to the ethical dimension of their work
- to serve as a tool in professional education.

These ideas are also applicable to codes of ethics relevant to other mental health professions.

In other words, codes of ethics identify what a professional body considers to be good practice. Many aspects of what constitutes good practice will depend on individual circumstances. The professional codes of ethics can help practitioners to identify what issues they need to consider for making a responsible and morally preferable decision. The codes of ethics do not typically identify a right or wrong solution to the problem at hand. Only in exceptional cases do they prescribe that a course of action is clearly 'right'. These exceptional cases relate to issues that the profession considers to be of great ethical concern and in need of systematic change. A sexual relationship between a psychiatrist and his or her client, for example, has been identified as a relationship that is not permitted. The profession considers sexual relationships with clients or former clients to be unethical (Australian Psychological Society, 2007, C.4.3).

However, codes of ethics are generally not prescriptive, focusing instead on the values that are integral to making an ethically well-considered decision. While codes of ethics do not prescribe one absolute way of how to behave, they aim to encourage practitioners to think about the right courses of action. One of the challenges for drafters of professional codes of ethics is to translate good practice into clearly understandable terminology. For example, a term such as 'autonomy', which is fundamental in medical ethics, evokes different understandings in different disciplines. Codes of ethics typically explain what 'respect for autonomy' means in practice; for example, for obtaining informed consent. The codes raise practitioners' awareness as to the multiple dimensions of their actions and explain, for example, why informed consent is not just a formality but an issue of moral importance. In particular, if codes of ethics are introduced through professional training, they serve as an educational tool for practitioners to understand the core values they express and to increase the understanding of professional rights and obligations.

By identifying professional standards of good practice, codes of ethics also serve as a benchmark for individual accountability and professional integrity. They help to establish whether an individual practitioner has met appropriate standards, and whether he or she should be subject to disciplinary action. To the world outside of the profession, individual misconduct also causes less damage to the reputation of the profession if there are clearly established ethical standards that members of the profession are expected to uphold. All Australian professional codes of ethics for mental health professionals acknowledge the importance of confidentiality, but do not consider it to be absolute.

Specific Codes of Ethics

The APS Code of Ethics (2007)

The Australian Psychological Society (APS) *Code of Ethics* (2007) sets out three fundamental principles that are relevant for understanding and applying the code. These fundamental ethical principles are the respect for the rights and dignity of the person, propriety and integrity, as expressed in its preamble. The preamble then links these three principles to other established principles of biomedical ethics: autonomy, justice, beneficence and non-maleficence. It states that respect for the rights and dignity of people and peoples 'includ[es] the right to autonomy and justice' and that propriety 'incorporates the principles of beneficence and non-maleficence' as well as 'responsibility to clients, the profession and society'. The principle of integrity is less directly concerned with biomedical ethics, but rather focuses on professional interests. It embraces the trust in, and reputation of, the discipline of psychology. The preamble states that the principle of integrity 'reflects the need for psychologists to have good character and acknowledges the high level of trust intrinsic to their professional relationships and impact of their conduct on the reputation of the profession'. However, there is an overlap between the three core principles, as respecting established bioethical principles will enhance the reputation of the profession.

The APS Code of Ethics sets out principles, which are accompanied by explanatory statements that help to understand how the principles are enacted (preamble). The code is also complemented by APS *Ethical Guidelines* for clarification and amplification (see preamble).

Under the heading of 'respect for the rights and dignity of people and peoples', *The APS Code of Ethics* outlines seven ethical standards. In its explanatory statement, the code recognises 'the importance of people's privacy and confidentiality'. Ethical Standard A.5 addresses confidentiality in further detail, clarifying that 'psychologists safeguard the confidentiality of information obtained during their provision of psychological services'. This encompasses the notion that psychologists 'make provisions for maintaining confidentiality' and that they 'take reasonable steps to protect the confidentiality of information' (A.5.1). Principle A.5.2 then sets out the following information:

> Psychologists ... disclose confidential information in
> the course of their provision of psychological services
> only under any one or more of the following circum-
> stances:
> (a) with the consent of the relevant client or a person
>   with legal authority to act on behalf of the client;
> (b) where there is a legal obligation to do so;
> (c) if there is an immediate and specified risk of
>   harm to an identifiable person or persons that
>   can be averted only by disclosing the informa-
>   tion; or
> (d) when consulting colleagues, or in the course of
>   supervision or professional training, provided the
>   psychologist:
>   (i) conceals the identity of clients and associated
>   parties involved; or
>   (ii) obtains the client's consent, and gives prior
>   notice to the recipients of the information that
>   they are required to preserve the client's pri-
>   vacy, and obtains an undertaking from the
>   recipients of the information that they will
>   preserve the client's privacy.

The subsequent paragraph (A.5.3) provides that psychologists
'inform their *clients* at the outset of the *professional relationship*,
and as regularly thereafter as is reasonably necessary, of (a) the
limits of confidentiality; and (b) the foreseeable uses of the information generated in the course of the relationship.' The code further clarifies that when it allows psychologists to disclose
information, psychologists 'disclose only that information which is
necessary to achieve the purpose of the disclosure, and then only
to people required to have that information' (A.5.4). Lastly, it
states that psychologists:

> use information collected about a client for a purpose
> other than the primary purpose of collection only:
> (a) with the consent of that client;
> (b) if the information is de-identified and used in the
>   course of duty approved research; or
> (c) when the use is required or authorised by or
>   under law. (A.5.5)

The APS' complementary *Guidelines on Confidentiality* (2007) further elaborates on professional confidentiality. It re-emphasises that confidentiality is 'a fundamental aspect of professional practice and is considered a cornerstone of the profession' (para 2.1). However, under the heading of 'limits to confidentiality' it also states that '[c]onfidentiality is not absolute' and that certain occasions 'may require that information ... be shared among relevant others including professional and family members, such as gathering an informant history for a neuropsychological assessment, or giving feedback to next of kin' (para 5.1). Disclosures of these kinds 'should be conveyed and explained to *clients*' (para 5.1). It elaborates, however, that these circumstances do not automatically result in a duty to disclose confidential information. Rather, a duty to disclose confidential information only exists 'when psychologists are legally obliged to disclose *client* information' (para 5.4). Some specific examples are given, such as reporting child abuse and neglect according to some state legislation, and reporting information that affects the security of the country. However, *Guidelines on Confidentiality* reminds psychologists to be mindful of the legal requirements of their workplace settings and advises psychologists that it is possible to react to a subpoena by seeking to vary it in consultation with the court (paras 5.4.1 and 5.4.2).

When psychologists are legally allowed to disclose information but are not compelled to do so, the decision whether to disclose confidential information is a matter of professional judgement (para 5.5.1). This applies in particular to situations that involve determining a 'risk, harm or danger to the *client* or others, which is sometimes referred to as the duty to warn or the duty to protect or care for the *client* and for others' (para 5.5.1). *Guidelines on Confidentiality* acknowledges (para 5.5.1) that:

> Dilemmas emerge when the need to maintain
> confidentiality competes with the duty to warn or
> to protect others. Part of the difficulty is associated
> with the definition and extent of the risk or harm
> and hence who ought to be protected. Some of the
> issues that need to be considered when making a
> professional judgement are presented in Section 5
> of the Guidelines for Working with People who
> Pose a High Risk of Harming Others (2005).

If psychologists decide to disclose information to third parties, the *Guidelines on Confidentiality* advise them to inform their clients about the following:

    (i)   [the fact that] information is to be disclosed;
    (ii) what information is to be disclosed;
    (iii) of the circumstances and the reasons for the intended disclosure of information; and
    (iv) to whom and when the disclosure is to be made.
    (para 5.5.2).

This, however, only applies 'where safety permits' the psychologist to inform their client (para 5.5.2).

The APS' complementary *Guidelines for Working with People Who Pose a High Risk of Harming Others* (2005) advises psychologists to keep up to date with structured and systematic risk assessment as well as be aware of the limitations of knowledge and skill in this area (para 1.3). It states that '[e]thical decision making with regard to problems of dangerous behaviour will often involve weighing up the level of risk and the duty of care towards potential victims against a client's right to confidentiality' (para 1.4). It further advises psychologists to 'act with due regard for the special competencies of other professionals' (para 3.1) and to thoroughly assess the level of risk while being mindful of their levels of expertise (para 3.3). However, it acknowledges that in 'an urgent situation, a psychologist with limited specialised knowledge or skill should do what is possible to avert or reduce harm where no greater level of expertise is available' and that it is 'appropriate to engage police intervention in such circumstances' (para 4.2). It draws attention to special circumstances such as matters involving alleged or perceived risks and matters involving children or persons with vulnerabilities (paras 5.4, 5.5, 5.8). It also outlines what should be discussed with clients who have reported their 'own dangerous behaviour' or acts of violence perpetrated against them by others (paras 5.6, 5.7).

Additionally, the APS has published further ethical guidelines on specific topics. In particular, *Guidelines on Reporting Child Abuse and Neglect, and Criminal Activity* (2003), *Guidelines on Record Keeping* (2004) and *Guidelines Relating to Suicidal Clients* (2004) are relevant in this context. All guidelines that pre-date *The APS Code of Ethics* (2007) are, however, subject to review.

The RANZCP Code of Ethics (2004)

The Royal Australian and New Zealand College of Psychiatrists' (RANZCP) *Code of Ethics* (2004) is less specific than *The APS Code of Ethics*, but it also includes a section on confidentiality. Principle 4 of *The RANZCP Code of Ethics* provides that '[p]sychiatrists shall strive to maintain patient confidentiality'. It acknowledges that 'in view of the particularly sensitive nature of patient information, psychiatrists have a special responsibility to maintain confidentiality' (Principle 4.1). It elaborates further, stating that striving to maintain confidentiality requires staying up-to-date with changes in information technology and organisational structures to enable professionals to properly store and take reasonable steps to safeguard patient information (Principle 4.2). The code specifies that 'information about the patient from sources other than the patient is subject to the same principles of confidentiality' (Principle 4.2).

The RANZCP Code of Ethics then explicitly clarifies that 'confidentiality cannot be absolute' (Principle 4.5). If disclosure of confidential information is considered, '[a] careful balance must be maintained between preserving confidentiality and the need to breach it in order to promote the best interests and safety of the patient and the safety and welfare of other persons' (Principle 4.5). The code permits the disclosure of confidential information by stating that '[p]sychiatrists may disclose confidential information if their patient intends to harm an identified person or persons' (Principle 4.6). In such cases '[p]sychiatrists may have an overriding duty to inform the intended victim(s) and/or the relevant authorities (Principle 4.6). Further, patients 'should be informed of the limits of confidentiality' from the beginning of the therapeutic relationship 'as part of the process of obtaining consent' (Principle 4.7). The code then clarifies that 'psychiatrists must act within the constraints of the law', but 'should question the need for disclosure or argue for only limited disclosure in legal proceedings' (Principle 4.8). If disclosure is required, the psychiatrist 'shall seek to divulge only what is relevant, strive to separate fact from opinion and avoid unnecessary speculation' (Principle 4.9). Finally, when psychiatrists breach confidentiality they 'must be able to justify their actions' (Principle 4.10).

The AASW Code of Ethics (2002)

The Australian Association of Social Workers' (AASW) *Code of Ethics* (2002) addresses information privacy and confidentiality at Principle 4.2.5. It provides that '[s]ocial workers will respect the right of clients to a relationship of trust, to privacy and confidentiality of their information and to responsible use of information obtained in the course of professional service'. The *AASW Code of Ethics* includes advice on how to introduce privacy and confidentiality to clients.

One important piece of advice is that social workers should inform their clients of the limits of confidentiality at the commencement of the professional relationship (Principle 4.2.5(b)). If social workers have to communicate clients' confidences, the *AASW Code of Ethics* provides that social workers shall communicate it only to 'appropriate personnel, either in the client's presence or with their informed consent' (Principle 4.2.5(d)). Therefore, disclosure should be limited to the specific purpose. The code further states that without the client's consent, confidential information 'may be revealed' when 'compelling ethical or legal reasons prevail' (Principle 4.2.5(d)). This includes fulfilling 'legal or statutory requirements' or 'to protect clients, other individuals or the public where the practitioner becomes aware that there is a risk to the client's safety or that of others' (Principle 4.2.5(d)(i)). The code states, however, that the risk must be carefully assessed, preferably in consultation with other professionals (Principle 4.2.5(d)(ii)). If confidential information of clients is used for other purposes, such as presentations, consultations, teaching, research or education, the information must be de-identified (Principle 4.2.5(g)).

Occupational Therapists' Code of Ethics (2001)

The *Code of Ethics* (2001) of the Australian Association of Occupational Therapists is founded on the bioethical principles of beneficence, non-maleficence, honesty, veracity, confidentiality, justice, respect and autonomy (Introductory Statement). It distinguishes between 'relationships with, and responsibilities to, patients and clients' and 'professional integrity', 'professional relationships and responsibilities' and 'professional standards'. Under the section entitled 'relationships with, and responsibilities to, patients and clients', it first addresses confidentiality. It states that '(b)eyond the necessary sharing of information with professional colleagues, occupational therapists are to safeguard confidential information relating to patients and clients' (p. 3). It clarifies that disclosure of confidential information is permitted when 'there is a legal compulsion' or when 'a patient/client gives informed consent' (p. 3). It also draws occupational therapists' attention to the legislation relating to access to information and names — Freedom of Information legislation — as an example (p. 3). In the section on professional standards, the code addresses record keeping and states that occupational therapists need to provide for the secure and confidential storage and disposal of records. They also need to be aware of the relevant legislation on access to personal information (p. 7).

Summary

In summary, it is noteworthy that each of these professional codes of ethics for mental health professionals acknowledges the importance of confidentiality, but does not consider it to be absolute. *The APS Code of Ethics* provides the most detail on how to deal with confidential information. Its framework on how to behave and how to guide decision-making derives from fundamental ethical principles. The principle-based approach to ethics was discussed in chapter 2 (p. 19ff).

The codes of ethics of the APS, the RANZCP and the AASW all state that patients or clients should be informed from the beginning of the therapeutic relationship that maintaining confidentiality is limited. Also, if disclosure seems likely to happen, they state that disclosure should be well-assessed, be limited as to its contents as well as to the persons receiving confidential information and be well-reasoned as to why particular information was revealed to whom.

Key Points

- All of the most relevant codes of ethics for mental health professionals stress the importance of maintaining confidentiality.
- All of these codes allow for disclosure in a range of circumstances. They vary in detail, but broadly summarised they allow disclosure:
  - with the client or patient's consent
  - if it is authorised or required by law
  - if it involves cases of child abuse, neglect or criminal activity
  - if there are certain risks of harm to self or others
  - if it is within the scope of providing treatment
  - if it is for a certain limited use for research, statistics and training.
- The codes also address:
  - how to approach informing a client or patient about the limits of confidentiality from the outset and when disclosure seems to become real
  - the ability of mental health professionals to facilitate, or argue for, limited disclosure
  - how to best keep information confidential
  - the need for mental health professionals to thoroughly assess and provide reasons for the disclosure.

Points of Reflection

- Be prepared that during your career you are likely to face a situation where you have to consider breaching confidentiality.
- Be aware of, and up to date with, the ethical standards of your profession and their interpretation. Try to identify which underlying values they aim to protect.
- Reflect on the ways in which your ethical approach is consistent with the ethical approach of your profession.
- Familiarise yourself with the content of your respective profession's ethical guidance, not just in relation to matters of confidentiality but also as to its rationale, values and principles.
- Clearly identify whether you have personal discrepancies and be constantly aware of them in your practice.

- If the ethical standards of your profession are not sufficiently clear to guide you, think about the underlying values they protect and try to apply them consistently to the circumstances of your case. Remember to distinguish your personal ethics from professional ethics, if there are discrepancies.

- Establish at least an informal network of colleagues with whom you can discuss ways to resolve ethical dilemmas, hypothetically and in practice. Reconsider your ethical standing in light of these discussions and learn to know who you could consult easily and quickly, if a conflict were to arise in practice.

- Be aware that going against the ethical standards of your profession is a clear indicator that you are acting unprofessionally as well as unethically. It is likely to be the end of your career.

- If you find yourself in a position where you are unsure whether to breach a client's confidentiality or where you consider violating professional ethics, consult with colleagues or a lawyer first.

- If there is an emergency, be prepared to explain in what ways you had to adjust your decision-making to the situation.

- If you have to reflect on your position, adopt a well-considered and systematic approach:

  - If the ethical guidance of your profession is not sufficiently precise, look into other mental health professionals' ethical standards and consider in what ways they would support your standing and why they would do so.

  - Clearly identify the possible conflicting interests you have considered and assess in what ways the individual circumstances of the case modify your options.

  - Clarify on what grounds you are making your decision and why that decision serves interests that are recognised as moral values. Always consider the impact of your decision on you personally, the client or patient, the profession, other people and the public in general.

Once you have familiarised yourself with the ethical framework for your practice and thoroughly reflected on it, it will be easier for you to assess a situation that becomes ethically challenging in practice.

CHAPTER 4

The Legal Framework for Protecting Confidentiality

This chapter focuses on laws relating to the protection of confidential information. The next two chapters look at laws enabling disclosure of confidential information in certain circumstances.

In order to comply with current laws, mental health professionals need to understand how and to what degree the law protects confidential information. In Australia, the legal protection of confidentiality is complex and confusing as it developed not only through the common law (judge-made law) but also through a variety of legislation. It can also involve matters of civil law and other forms of public law, including regulatory law relating to the mental health professions.

Each Australian state and territory has its own mental health legislation. However the states and territories also share the regulation of health care with the Commonwealth. This means that in addition to the state-based mental health legislation, other important legal provisions exist. For example, each of the nine different jurisdictions has provisions on how to deal with health information. These provisions can be found both in a federal privacy scheme and in the state and territory health records and information privacy legislation. On an even broader level, there are legal provisions that are unrelated to health but are applicable to at least some individuals working in mental health care. These different provisions all interrelate and tie in with the common law. Their understanding is also influenced by overseas case law and increasingly important human rights arguments.

This chapter will begin with a basic description of how the law developed with regard to the protection of confidential information. It will first assess this development in the civil law as this provides a basic understanding of many relevant legal aspects of confidentiality in therapeutic relationships. In doing so, it will canvas the laws of contracts, torts and equity, which are the predominant legal foundations for breach of confidentiality claims. This discussion will include references to relevant sections of the civil liability legislation.

This chapter will also set out some basic statutory requirements for maintaining confidentiality. As the scope of mental health care is very broad, many of the relevant statutory specifications are intertwined in different pieces of legislation that apply to certain categories of working in the mental health sector. A comprehensive discussion of these specifications would be rather confusing, and statutory provisions in areas such as handling and storing health information are subject to constant legislative change. Consequently, some areas of statutory law will be addressed in basic terms only and the overview will focus on introducing a general understanding of the federal privacy scheme as well as state and territory legislation concerning mental health, health records and information privacy.

The final section deals briefly with regulatory law relating to the mental health professions.

The Legal Protection of Confidentiality

An important premise with regard to law and confidentiality is that the law generally protects confidential information in therapeutic relationships. Thus, in principle, the law requires mental health professionals to maintain confidentiality.

The legal protection of confidentiality has evolved through common law jurisprudence. Judges have not yet exhaustively defined the legal nature of a duty to preserve confidentiality, but they have accepted that such a duty exists for health professionals, including psychiatrists and psychologists. The origins of a duty to preserve confidentiality can be found in the laws of contracts, torts and equity, which will be discussed in turn. The manner in which confidentiality is protected, and to what extent, varies in these different areas of law, significantly affecting the nature of each claim.

Contract Law
When Does a Contract Exist?

The general protection of confidentiality predominately originates from the law of contracts. In private health care, the doctor–patient relationship is typically based on a contract between the parties, and maintaining confidential information has been recognised as a contractual obligation (*Kadian v Richards* (2004) 61 NSWLR 222 at 241; *Hunter v Mann* [1974] QB 767 at 772; *Parry-Jones v Law Society* [1969] 1 Ch 1 at 7 and 9; *Breen v Williams* (1996) 186 CLR 71 at 102f). It is not necessary for the health professional and the client or patient to sign a written contract or to agree on all terms of treatment and payment in order to enter contractual obligations. What is relevant is that both parties — expressly or impliedly — agree, consider and intend to enter a legally binding relationship (Devereux, 2007, p. 139). The demands are not high when it comes to assessing whether the parties have agreed, considered and intended to enter into contractual obligations; it is usually sufficient that a client or patient seeks treatment from a mental health professional who then offers help and expects payment for that service.

The nature of the relationship may be complicated if a health professional is employed by a hospital, health care centre or similar service, or if a third party such as Medicare commonly pays for the patient's or client's treatment. However, this does not necessarily obliterate the contractual basis of the relationship.

A contractual relationship with the client or patient does not exist, however, when the mental health professional assumes a relationship with that client or patient for the reason of issuing a report on their mental health.

What Does the Contract Say About Confidentiality?

Once a contract has been established between the health care professional and his or her client or patient, it is important to consider whether the contract includes implied or express terms of confidentiality. Implied terms of a contract are terms that are inherently necessary for the contract to exist, or terms that a party to the contract reasonably expects considering the nature, type or class of the contract (*Breen v Williams* (1996) 186 CLR 71 at 102–103). The common law has accepted that there is a reasonable expectation that information between doctors and their patients remains confidential and that a duty to preserve confidentiality is generally implied in the contract between doctor and patient (*Duncan v Medical Practitioners Disciplinary Committee* [1986] 1 NZLR 513 at 520; *Furniss v Fitchett* [1958] NZLR 396 at 399). In *Parry-Jones v Law Society* [1969] 1 Ch 1 at 7, Lord Denning stated: 'The law implies a term into the contract whereby a professional man [or woman] is to keep his [or her] client's affairs secret and not to disclose them to anyone without just cause'. Although this statement directly concerned the relationship between a lawyer and client, Lord Denning applied this contractually implied duty to preserve confidentiality to other professional relationships. He explicitly included the doctor–patient relationship (*Parry-Jones v Law Society* [1969] 1 Ch 1 at 7).

As reflected in Lord Denning's statement, there are just causes for disclosing confidential information. Indeed, the common law has established that the promise of confidentiality is not absolute. In what ways the protection of confidentiality is limited will be further addressed in chapter 5. The main problem relating to a duty to preserve confidentiality is to define its scope. For example, can a client or patient still expect confidentiality when he or she admits to neglecting their child? Or is there a reasonable expectation that this admission would fall outside of a general expectation of confidentiality? There is little case law or other guidance on how to define the current reasonable expectation. When deciding to what degree a client or patient would expect confidentiality, the court will consider established legal principles, what an ordinary contract would include and what the individual parties would have agreed upon in the given circumstances (*Breen v Williams* (1996) 186 CLR 71 at 102 per Gaudron and McHugh JJ).

Express terms can diverge from implied terms. If mental health professionals and their clients or patients have a written or oral agreement on details of their contractual relationship, that agreement is binding. However, some contractual agreements can be void; for example, when they are based on a mutual error or when they involve committing a crime or tort. (These are, however, rather atypical and rather obvious exclusions.) Thus, the parties to the contract can modify the terms of the contract and can choose to depart from what is expressly in the contract.

Clarifying the extent to which a mental health professional is obliged to maintain confidentiality is central to assessing matters of liability. It is for this reason that mental health professionals are advised to discuss matters of confidentiality at the outset of the therapeutic relationship. An express term can clarify the circumstances in which a mental health professional's obligation to maintain confidentiality ceases. It provides a more concrete framework for deciding whether or not the mental health professional actually breached confidentiality. At the same time, it can clarify in what manner a mental health professional might provide information to third parties, and it may also name those third parties.

If the agreement is not sufficiently precise to become part of the contract, discussing how to deal with confidential information can at least clarify for the client or patient in what circumstances he or she cannot expect confidentiality. Even a general discussion, conveying that there might be cases in which the mental health professional will have to disclose confidential information and outlining what those circumstances could be, gives the client or patient an idea of where a contractual duty to maintain confidentiality might end. A mental health professional can, for example, discuss at the outset of a consultation whether the client or patient wishes the mental health professional to inform relatives or family if the mental health of the client or patient deteriorates.

Given that maintaining confidentiality is important for professional practice and ethics, discussing the limitations of confidentiality with a client or patient must be a well-balanced exercise. It should not be seen purely as a cautious protection from liability.

The extent to which confidentiality should be limited is dependent on the scope of practice. While confidentiality is central to mental health care, some mental health areas are inherently limited in providing confidential services, such as forensic mental health services. In these cases, it is advisable to explicitly address the limits of confidentiality. Other mental health professionals may have greater flexibility to address matters of confidentiality depending on how the therapeutic relationship evolves and whether reporting duties seem likely to arise.

Discussing Confidentiality at the Beginning of the Therapeutic Relationship

It is important to establish realistic expectations around confidentiality. One way of striking the balance between assuring confidentiality and clarifying its limitations is to start with a basic explanation:

- the client or patient should understand that confidentiality will be generally protected;
- the client or patient should be informed that there might be circumstances in which confidential information will have to be disclosed; and
- the client or patient should have a basic understanding of what these circumstances could be.

Use examples, if necessary.

The manner in which confidentiality should be addressed and the degree to which limitations should be discussed are best to be adjusted to the individual circumstances of the case, such as:

- the reasons why the client or patient seeks or receives mental health services;
- the degree of mental health concerns; and
- the scope and the realities of the mental health service provided.

It could be useful to indicate whether the branch of mental health service typically comes with frequent or rare instances in which confidentiality cannot be maintained.

If a mental health professional works in an environment in which they inevitably have powers of control, monitoring or restriction, they will have to address with the client or patient in what ways they might have to exercise these powers at the cost of maintaining confidentiality.

In private practice, mental health professionals will have greater flexibility, but they should prepare their clients or patients for the fact that they will, or might have to, share some information; for example, when they give information to others who are involved in a client's or patient's care or treatment, or if they have to report certain, severe matters, such as child abuse or certain intended crimes or threats to others.

How to Integrate an Initial Discussion on Confidentiality into Daily Practice

One way of integrating an initial discussion on confidentiality into daily practice is to establish a systematic approach to discussing confidentiality with the client or patient. In different areas of mental health services, mental health professionals should reflect on what it means in their practice to deal with confidential information. In turn, establishing a systematic approach to introducing confidentiality to clients and patients should reflect:

• the mental health professional's usual practice;

• what the client or patient usually expects from the therapeutic relationship; and

• how the mental health professional usually approaches his or her clients or patients in regard to confidentiality.

Such an approach should be scrutinised as to why that approach seems to be working and whether it complies with current ethical and legal standards.

In the individual circumstances this approach can also be adjusted according to the scope of the mental health service, the nature of the therapeutic relationship and the character of the client or patient. For example, the actions of the mental health professional should reflect whether the character of the client or patient calls for a more careful approach to guaranteeing confidentiality or to expressing its limitations.

Mental health professionals are advised to make note in the health records of such an initial discussion on confidentiality as details in records will become relevant if questions of civil liability arise. If mental health professionals have established a well-considered, systematic approach to discussing confidentiality at the outset of the therapeutic relationship, their note taking could be made easier by recording in what ways they made adjustments to their general approach and why they did so.

What is Contractual Liability?

Contractual liability does not only depend on the extent to which confidentiality was guaranteed or expected. If information was disclosed and that disclosure was in conflict with the contractual agreement, civil liability also depends on whether the mental health professional exercised reasonable care and skill. Lord Denning acknowledged that a professional person who enters a professional contractual obligation warrants using reasonable care and skill (*Greaves & Co (Contractors) Ltd v Baynham, Meikle & Partners* [1975] 1 WLR 1095 at 1100). Thus, when a mental health professional has a duty to maintain confidentiality, he or she will not be liable for all disclosures that are made. Rather, whether the mental health professional provided confidential services with reasonable care and skill will be assessed.

Again, the question arises as to what is reasonable practice. The common law has addressed the question of what is reasonable care and skill, mainly in the law of torts. Some of these ideas are also applicable to the law of contracts and they will be further addressed subsequently.

Key Points

- When a mental health professional and a client or patient assume a therapeutic relationship, they typically enter a contractual relationship.
- The law recognises that a client or patient reasonably expects confidential health services and it generally protects that expectation. If matters of confidentiality are not discussed, the law implies a term into the contract that a health professional has a duty to maintain confidentiality.
- Explicitly discussing matters of confidentiality can modify what the client or patient may reasonably expect, and it can modify the extent of the mental health professional's duty to maintain confidentiality.
- In order to establish realistic expectations, mental health professionals should explicitly discuss confidentiality at the outset of each therapeutic relationship. The client or patient should understand

that confidentiality will be generally protected, but he or she needs to be made aware that there might be circumstances in which confidential information will have to be disclosed. He or she should also have a basic understanding of what these circumstances could be.

- The degree to which limitations should be explicitly addressed and the manner in which this ought to be conveyed should be guided by practical experience. It should also be adjusted to the scope of the mental health service, the nature of the therapeutic relationship and the character of the client or patient.

- The mental health professional should take note of how he or she approaches matters of confidentiality when first consulting with a new client or patient. It is helpful to follow a systematic approach to talking with the client or patient about confidentiality and to make note of whether the first consultation with a new client or patient followed that approach, or if not, in what ways it derived from it and why.

Points of Reflection

- Try to establish a systematic approach for addressing confidentiality at the beginning of a new therapeutic relationship. Consider the nature of your relationship with the client or patient and try to imagine what he or she would expect from the kind of service you provide. Should that expectation be limited?

- Take note of your first consultation with each client or patient. Did you talk about specific details or did you form any individual agreements?

- Try to convey the reality of your practice and use your practical experience to explain to the client or patient what he or she can realistically expect from the service you provide.

- Use your practical experience to strike a balance between assuring a confidential service and clarifying its limitations.

- Reconsider your approach in light of what you think has or has not worked in your experience.

Torts

What is a Claim in Torts?

The law of confidentiality also developed through the law of torts. This type of law is concerned with civil wrongs and includes the law of negligence. Typically, the relationship between a mental health professional and his or her client or patient is based on a contract. However, there are instances of service provision where there are no valid contractual bases, such as in forensic settings. Tort law does not require a contract between the parties; rather, it focuses on elements of trust and proximity within the relationship between the parties. Tort and contract law are not mutually exclusive, but they are different areas of law with different requirements. Given that there can be overlap between the two, a client or patient can be in a position to make a claim in tort law and in the law of contracts. In general, a claim in tort law requires that a duty of care between the parties has been breached and that the breach caused damage that was reasonably foreseeable.

The common law has established a duty of care between health care providers and their patients or clients due to the nature of their relationship and the close proximity between them (McIlwraith & Madden, 2006, p. 171ff). In *Furniss v Fitchett* [1959] NZLR 396 at 405, Barrowclough J stated: '[F]rom the very nature of the communications which customarily pass from a patient to his or her medical advisers, the latter stands in a special and peculiar fiduciary duty to the former' (at 405; see also *A-G v Guardian Newspapers (No 2)* [1988] 3 All ER 545 at 639f).

Traditional fiduciary relationships exist between confidants and lawyers, priests, bankers and doctors (*Parry-Jones v Law Society* [1969] 1 Ch 1 at 7), although the legal protection of these different professional relationships varies. Importantly, these relationships all bear an element of trust that is so widely recognised in society that the confider does not reasonably expect disclosure.

What is Reasonable Care and Skill?

Many questions arise as to the nature of the health professional's duty of care, whether there was a breach of that duty and whether there was a foreseeable risk involved. Determining whether a duty of care was breached is based on considerations of what a reasonable and ordinary skilled person of that profession would have done or assessed (*Bolam v Friern Hospital Management Committee* [1957] 2 All ER 118).

The *Bolam* decision established that the assessment of what is reasonable for a medical practitioner depends on what a 'respectable', 'reasonable' and 'responsible body of medical men skilled in that particular art' would accept as a standard of 'practice accepted as proper' (at [122] per McNair J). This assessment was subsequently applied and interpreted in a way that was restrictive for courts. Once experts testified that a course of action was a 'proper' course of action according to their standards, courts had little scope to evaluate whether expert opinion was rational or reasonable. Even if there was conflicting expert opinion, judicial scrutiny was reduced to finding out whether there was expert opinion that supported the view that the action complied with proper professional standards, regardless of whether that was a minority opinion. Applying this standard in such a way ran the risk of doctors setting their own standards as giving expert testimony was treated as conclusive of whether or not an action was negligent (Manning, 2007, p. 397). However, there have been two important modifications to this standard.

The case of *Rogers v Whitaker* (1992) 175 CLR 479 modified what advice and information should be given by health professionals to their patients in order to obtain informed consent. The High Court of Australia decided that assessing what is reasonable care and skill was no longer a matter of medical judgement only. Chief Justice Mason and Justices Brennan, Dawson, Toohey and McHugh stated:

> [P]articularly in the field of non-disclosure of risk and the provision of advice and information, the Bolam principle has been discarded and, instead, the courts have adopted the principle that, while evidence of acceptable medical practice is a useful guide for the courts, it is for the courts to adjudicate on what is the appropriate standard of care after giving weight to 'the paramount consideration that a person is entitled to make his own decisions about his life'. (at 484; further references omitted)

This decision demonstrates an important shift towards respect for patients' rights: the High Court gave 'paramount consideration' to an individual's right to autonomy and self-determination. It decided that a professional standard of reasonable care and skill is not only guided by professional experts, but also by the patient and a respect for patients' rights. Thus, when judges decide what is reasonable care and skill, they will be guided by expert opinion, but they will also give significant weight to the rights of the affected person when considering what action was appropriate. The increasing importance of human rights arguments within Australian law underpins this position.

The second important modification to the assessment of professional standards came with the case of *Bolitho v City & Hackney Health Authority* [1998] AC 232. This case considered whether the diagnosis and treatment of a patient was exercised with reasonable care and skill. It clarified that expert opinion must be 'capable of withstanding logical analysis' (at 243 per Lord Browne-Wilkinson) and that it must involve weighing risks and benefits to the patient. Lord Browne-Wilkinson noted:

> (T)he judge before accepting a body of opinion as
> being responsible, reasonable or respectable, will
> need to be satisfied that, in forming their views, the
> experts have directed their mind to the question of
> comparative risks and benefits and have reached a
> defensible conclusion on the matter. (at 241)

Thus, Lord Browne-Wilkinson modified the *Bolam* decision, allowing for judicial scrutiny over whether expert testimony is inappropriate. However, in the process of clarifying this, Judge Browne-Wilkinson (at 243) estimated that medical expert opinion will only be held to be inappropriate in rare cases. Subsequent case law confirms that courts are indeed reluctant to condemn expert opinion (Manning, 2007, p. 399).

In an effort to establish nationally consistent torts legislation, Australian torts law has been under reform since 2002. The Review Committee recommended that Australian civil liability legislation should take on a standard of assessment similar to the one in the *Bolitho* decision. They recommended: '[a] medical practitioner is not negligent, if the treatment provided was in accordance with an opinion widely held by a significant number of respected practitioners in the field, unless the court considers that opinion was irrational' (Ipp Committee Report, 2002, p. 1).

All Australian jurisdictions have incorporated civil liability legislation, most of which is newly introduced or recently reformed, into their statutory regimes: *Civil Law (Wrongs) Act 2002* (ACT); *Civil Liability Act 2002* (NSW); *Personal Injuries (Liabilities and Damages) Act 2003* (NT); *Civil Liability Act 2003* (Qld); *Civil Liability Act 1936* (SA); *Civil Liability Act 2002* (Tas); *Wrongs Act 1958* (Vic); *Civil Liability Act 2002* (WA). These Acts comply to varying degrees with the Review Committee's recommendations, but they have all adopted the suggested Bolam-modified test, which now applies to all professions (Ipp, 2007, p. 458; Kerridge et al., 2009, p. 139). The new and revised legislation now clarifies general principles of a duty of care and outlines what elements will be considered when determining whether a person was negligent. According to the new standard, a mental health professional is only negligent if:

- there was a foreseeable risk;
- the risk was 'not insignificant'; and
- in the circumstances, a reasonable person in the mental health professional's position would have taken precautions that the mental health professional did not take.

To answer the question of whether a reasonable person would have taken precautions, courts will now consider:

- the probability that harm would occur, if no precautions were taken;
- the likely seriousness of the harm;
- the burden of taking precautions to avoid the risk of harm; and
- whether there is a social utility in the activity that creates the risk of harm and what that social utility is.

Importantly, the new or reformed laws assess liability on the basis of expert opinion (what 'a reasonable person in the person's position' would do), unless that opinion is unreasonable or irrational. The details of what the terms 'unreasonable' and 'irrational' mean in the context of the new civil liability legislation will need to be further clarified by Australian courts.

The civil liability reforms also resulted in the following changes:

- The period in which negligence claims can be initiated has been shortened.
- Compensation has been limited and minimum thresholds for claims have been put into place.
- Exemplary and punitive damages for negligence can no longer be claimed.
- Damages for non-economic loss must meet a minimum threshold and they have been capped to a maximum sum of compensation.

Table 4.1 outlines the general principles on duties of care across Australian jurisdictions. The actual wording from the legislation is used.

Table 4.1
General Principles on Duties of Care in Civil Liability Legislation in Australian Jurisdictions

ACT: Civil Law (Wrongs) Act 2002

s 43 Precautions against risk — general principles

(1) A person is not negligent in failing to take precautions against a risk of harm unless —

    (a) the risk was foreseeable (that is, it is a risk of which the person knew or ought to have known); and

    (b) the risk was not insignificant; and

    (c) in the circumstances, a reasonable person in the person's position would have taken those precautions.

(2) In deciding whether a reasonable person would have taken precautions against a risk of harm, the court must consider the following (among other relevant things):

    (a) the probability that the harm would happen if precautions were not taken;

    (b) the likely seriousness of the harm;

    (c) the burden of taking precautions to avoid the risk of harm;

    (d) the social utility of the activity creating the risk of harm.

continued over

....

Table 4.1 (continued)
General Principles on Duties of Care in Civil Liability Legislation in Australian Jurisdictions

NSW: Civil Liability Act 2002 No.22

5B General principles

(1) A person is not negligent in failing to take precautions against a risk of harm unless:

  (a) the risk was foreseeable (that is, it is a risk of which the person knew or ought to have known), and

  (b) the risk was not insignificant, and

  (c) in the circumstances, a reasonable person in the person's position would have taken those precautions.

(2) In determining whether a reasonable person would have taken precautions against a risk of harm, the court is to consider the following (amongst other relevant things):

  (a) the probability that the harm would occur if care were not taken,

  (b) the likely seriousness of the harm,

  (c) the burden of taking precautions to avoid the risk of harm,

  (d) the social utility of the activity that creates the risk of harm.

NT: No equivalent provision.

Qld: Civil Liability Act 2003

9. General principles

(1) A person does not breach a duty to take precautions against a risk of harm unless —

  (a) the risk was foreseeable (that is, it is a risk of which the person knew or ought reasonably to have known); and

  (b) the risk was not insignificant; and

  (c) in the circumstances, a reasonable person in the position of the person would have taken the precautions.

(2) In deciding whether a reasonable person would have taken precautions against a risk of harm, the court is to consider the following (among other relevant things) —

  (a) the probability that the harm would occur if care were not taken;

  (b) the likely seriousness of the harm;

  (c) the burden of taking precautions to avoid the risk of harm;

  (d) the social utility of the activity that creates the risk of harm.

continued over

Table 4.1 (continued)
General Principles on Duties of Care in Civil Liability Legislation in Australian Jurisdictions

SA: Civil Liability Act 1936 No. 2267

s 32 Precautions against risk

(1) A person is not negligent in failing to take precautions against a risk of harm unless —

    (a) the risk was foreseeable (that is, it is a risk of which the person knew or ought to have known); and

    (b) the risk was not insignificant; and

    (c) in the circumstances, a reasonable person in the person's position would have taken those precautions.

(2) In determining whether a reasonable person would have taken precautions against a risk of harm, the court is to consider the following (amongst other relevant things):

    (a) the probability that the harm would occur if precautions were not taken;

    (b) the likely seriousness of the harm;

    (c) the burden of taking precautions to avoid the risk of harm;

    (d) the social utility of the activity that creates the risk of harm.

Tas: Civil Liability Act 2002 No. 54

11. General principles

(1) A person does not breach a duty to take reasonable care unless –

    (a) there was a foreseeable risk of harm (that is, a risk of harm of which the person knew or ought reasonably to have known); and

    (b) the risk was not insignificant; and

    (c) in the circumstances, a reasonable person in the position of the person would have taken precautions to avoid the risk.

(2) In deciding whether a reasonable person would have taken precautions against a risk of harm, the court is to consider the following (among other relevant things):

    (a) the probability that the harm would occur if care were not taken;

    (b) the likely seriousness of the harm;

    (c) the burden of taking precautions to avoid the risk of harm;

    (d) the potential net benefit of the activity that exposes others to the risk of harm.

(3) For the purpose of subsection (2)(c), the court is to consider the burden of taking precautions to avoid similar risks of harm for which the person may be responsible.

continued over

....

Table 4.1 (continued)
General Principles on Duties of Care in Civil Liability Legislation in Australian Jurisdictions

Vic: Wrongs Act 1958 No. 6420

48. General principles

(1) A person is not negligent in failing to take precautions against a risk of harm unless —

    (a) the risk was foreseeable (that is, it is a risk of which the person knew or ought to have known); and

    (b) the risk was not insignificant; and

    (c) in the circumstances, a reasonable person in the person's position would have taken those precautions.

(2) In determining whether a reasonable person would have taken precautions against a risk of harm, the court is to consider the following (amongst other relevant things) —

    (a) the probability that the harm would occur if care were not taken;

    (b) the likely seriousness of the harm;

    (c) the burden of taking precautions to avoid the risk of harm;

    (d) the social utility of the activity that creates the risk of harm.

(3) For the purposes of subsection (1)(b) —

    (a) insignificant risks include, but are not limited to, risks that are far-fetched or fanciful; and

    (b) risks that are not insignificant are all risks other than insignificant risks and include, but are not limited to, significant risks.

WA: Civil Liability Act 2002 No. 35

5B. General principles

(1) A person is not liable for harm caused by that person's fault in failing to take precautions against a risk of harm unless —

    (a) the risk was foreseeable (that is, it is a risk of which the person knew or ought to have known);

    (b) the risk was not insignificant; and

    (c) in the circumstances, a reasonable person in the person's position would have taken those precautions.

(2) In determining whether a reasonable person would have taken precautions against a risk of harm, the court is to consider the following (amongst other relevant things) —

    (a) the probability that the harm would occur if care were not taken;

    (b) the likely seriousness of the harm;

    (c) the burden of taking precautions to avoid the risk of harm;

    (d) the social utility of the activity that creates the risk of harm.

Note: All legislation is referred to as it applied on 1 August 2009.

What is Reasonable Care and Skill for Deciding Whether or Not to Disclose Confidential Information?

In deciding what is reasonable care and skill, judges will assess both medical and judicial standards of care. When looking at reasonable care and skill in relation to disclosure of confidential information, courts are likely to adopt an approach that reflects elements of both modifications to the *Bolam* decision. The *Rogers v Whitaker* case placed paramount consideration on a person's autonomy and his or her right to self-determination and privacy. As discussed earlier, respecting an individual's autonomy and their right to self-determination and privacy are fundamental grounds for maintaining confidentiality. Thus, it is likely that courts would measure reasonable care and skill by considering whether mental health professionals have 'reasonably' balanced clinical criteria with privacy considerations. With human rights values becoming increasingly embedded in Australian law, it is reasonable to expect courts to give special consideration to a person's self-determination when deciding who should know about confidential information.

Some further clarification can be derived from the common law. The High Court of Australia introduced a 'foreseeability test' with its decision in *Sullivan v Moody* (2001) 207 CLR 562. It stated that a foreseeable risk must be more than just a question of proximity and possibility:

> But the fact that [a harm] is foreseeable, in the sense of being a real and not far-fetched possibility, that a careless act or omission on the part of one person may cause harm to another does not mean that the first person is subject to a legal liability to compensate the second by way of damages for negligence if there is such carelessness, and harm results. If it were otherwise, at least two consequences would follow. First, the law would subject citizens to an intolerable burden of potential liability, and constrain their freedom of action in a gross manner. Secondly, the tort of negligence would subvert many other principles of law, and statutory provisions, which strike a balance of rights and obligations, duties and freedoms. A defendant will only be liable, in negligence, for failure

> to take reasonable care to prevent *a certain kind of
> foreseeable harm* to a plaintiff, in circumstances
> where the law imposes a duty to take such care. (at
> 200, emphasis added by the authors)

The foreseeability test set out in this case guides courts to 'look at issues such as the probability of the harm occurring and its significance, the costs of avoiding the harm and the social utility of the activity that gave rise to the injury' (Kerridge et al., 2009, p. 141). These clarifying aspects are now included in the state and territory civil liability legislation, which provides guidance to mental health professionals when deciding whether to disclose confidential information (see Table 4.1, p. 48ff).

A form of 'foreseeability test' can be used by mental health professionals in deciding whether to preserve confidentiality. For example, determining whether it is unreasonable for a mental health professional to disclose confidential information can be measured by whether he or she properly weighed the conflicting interests before reaching a decision. In other words, mental health professionals are advised to consider the impact of disclosing information against the impact of maintaining it. This consideration should show respect for an individual's fundamental rights and freedoms, but also balance possible risks and benefits to the client or patient or others. The 'irrationality/unreasonability' test can also be measured on the basis of established standards, such as professional practice and codes of ethics as well as legal provisions. These sources of information are a significant point of reference for scrutinising whether a course of action was irrational or unreasonable.

It is worth noting that mental health professionals do not generally have to prove the reasonability of their decisions. It is rare that judges actually question whether professional practice is reasonable, unless there are indicators to the contrary. Judicial scrutiny is also not measured on the basis of optimal practice. But in case professional practice is questioned, mental health professionals who ensure they comply with current ethics and law and who are prepared to reflect and reason their individual decision in light of these measures are in a good position to defend the reasonableness of their practice.

Key Points

- The law of torts protects certain relationships of trust, such as the one between psychiatrists or psychologists and their client or patient.
- The law of torts acknowledges that health professionals have a duty to maintain confidentiality with reasonable care and skill due to the nature of the relationship and the close proximity to their client or patient.
- What is reasonable care and skill will be measured on the basis of professional expertise, unless that expertise is unreasonable.
- Courts have found medical expert evidence unreasonable in a few cases only.
- The law has not yet clarified how to measure what is unreasonable. The reasonableness of a decision can be measured based on whether mental health professionals balance possible risks and benefits to the client or patient or others, and whether they comply with ethical and legal standards.
- One important reason why law and ethics protect confidentiality is to respect an individual's autonomy and his or her right to self-determination and privacy. Decisions on whether or not to disclose confidential information must start with the paramount consideration that these rights need to be carefully protected.

Points of Reflection

- Familiarise yourself with what is considered to be negligent according to the civil liability legislation of the state or territory in which your practice is located.
- Consider in what ways these considerations translate to your practice.
- Be aware that many of these considerations are practice-oriented and assessed by experts in your fields.
- Learn to reflect and reason your decision-making on the basis of what is reasonable care and skill for your profession.

Equity

The duty to maintain confidentiality is also relevant in the law of equity. Equity is a legal concept that protects good faith. It can be drawn upon to restrain someone from using information without authorisation, if the unauthorised use of information caused damage or is likely to cause damage. The law of equity protects the nature of confidential information itself (*Stephens v Avery* [1988] 2 All ER 477; *Campbell v MGN Ltd* [2004] UKHL 22), but the nature of the information must be so personal, private or intimate that the affected person has a reasonable expectation that the information would not be disclosed to others (*Campbell v MGN Ltd* [2004] UKHL 22). It is also relevant that the information was imparted in circumstances that give rise to an obligation of confidence (*Coco v AN Clark (Engineers) Ltd* (1968) 1A IPR 587 at 590; *Wainwright v Home Office* [2003] 3 WLR 1337 at [29]).

The law has recognised that the therapeutic relationship between a health professional and their client or patient is typically a fiduciary relationship in which the client or patient can reasonably expect confidentiality. Whether the relationship between health professional and client or patient is indeed fiduciary may need to be assessed on a case-by-case basis (see *Breen v Williams* (1994) 35 NSWLR 522; Herdy, 1996). The common law has also recognised that losing trust in confidential health services is a sufficient basis on which to argue for damage (*Ashworth v MGN Ltd* [2001] 1 All ER 191).

The law of equity offers strong protection with regard to confidential information. In comparison to the law of contracts and torts, a claim in equity is the most straightforward and most easily enforceable claim for someone claiming a breach in confidentiality. The explicit or implied terms of a contract do not need to be considered and a claim in equity does not rest on the uncertain task of interpreting what is reasonable care and skill with respect to maintaining confidentiality.

However, claims in equity are limited in their outcome. The main remedy of a claim in equity is an injunction. However, clients or patients will not usually know that their confidentiality has been breached until it is already too late. Thus, equity's focus on preventing someone from revealing confidential information will not be of much help for clients or patients who already suffered from their confidential information being disclosed. Equity does reward damages as well, but the damages that have been rewarded in equity have been very low (*Cornelius v De Taranto* [2001] 68 BMLR 62). Thus, claims in equity are fairly unlikely. As the therapeutic relationship is typically based on a contract and is recognised as a fiduciary relationship in torts law, claims in contract law or torts law seem to be more likely, despite involving more uncertainties.

There are nonetheless a few instances where claims in equity are of particular relevance. For example, equity can be applied to cases in which the relevant information is in the hands of third persons or cases in which confidential information directly affects or involves persons other than the doctor and patient. Thus, claims in equity are particularly important when confidential information gets lost or used by others, such as when unauthorised persons gain access to health records.

Key Points

- The law of equity protects the good faith a person places in having his or her confidential information kept confidential.
- Claims in equity focus on injunctions, to prevent someone from disclosing confidential information.
- There is limited scope to claim damages in equity.
- Claims in equity are important when confidential information gets lost or used by third parties.

The Limitations of Civil Law Claims

The laws of contracts, torts and equity fall within a general category of 'civil' law. Claims in civil law focus on compensation. If confidential information is disclosed to third parties, a client or patient can sue the mental health professional for malpractice and claim compensation as damages. However, such claims have requirements that are not easy for clients or patients to prove, and successful claims are rare.

In civil matters, the burden of proof is typically on the claimant and the standard of proof is less strict than in criminal matters. The client or patient usually does not need to give proof beyond reasonable doubt; rather, a balance of probabilities is sufficient. This means that courts will consider what is more probable than not (Travers, 2002, p. 259, with further references). In order to form an opinion on what is more probable, courts will apply common sense and consider past experiences, expert testimony and ideas of possibility and probability (Travers, 2002, p. 258f). Thus, for example, the claimant does not need to prove the exact terms of a contract. Instead, the court can find what was probably the content of the contract after considering the terms that are typically contained in a contract, the usual practice of the mental health professional and the individual circumstances of the case.

Nevertheless, it is difficult for the client or patient to prove the elements of a civil claim. Certain terms such as what can be 'reasonably expected' or what is 'reasonable care and skill' are open to interpretation and the law does not provide clear insight into what these terms mean in the context of a therapeutic setting. In the contractual relationship between a mental health professional and his or her client or patient, two elements are typically open to interpretation: assessing to what extent the mental health professional has a contractual obligation to maintain confidentiality, and assessing whether the mental health professional exercised that obligation with reasonable care and skill. Equally, claims in the law of torts depend on whether the mental health professional had a duty of care and whether he or she behaved outside of what is deemed to be a standard of reasonable care and skill.

These legal uncertainties are coupled with factual difficulties as breaches in confidentiality do not typically result in measurable damages. It is difficult to measure the embarrassment caused when confidential information is revealed in terms of financial loss or injury. This factor combined with the risk of having to bear the costs of an unsuccessful claim, the stress of going through the procedure and the inherent vulnerabilities for a client or patient, means that clients and patients are unlikely to make successful civil claims. Loane Skene (2008) comments that there have been only a few common law cases dealing with breaches of confidentiality. She estimates that even less will appear now that there is an option to seek compensation through a complaint to the privacy health commissioner (p. 272).

Disciplinary Law

Claiming a breach of confidentiality is also possible through laws regulating the mental health professions (here referred to as disciplinary law), which is a part of administrative law. Disciplinary law focuses on matters of discipline and investigates wrongful conduct. It can result in a professional being ordered to have further training, supervision or similar. It can also result in fines as well as the suspension or cancellation of a professional licence. The procedure is in the hands of a regulatory body and its purpose is to protect the integrity and reputation of the profession.

In contrast to a civil liability claim, there is no minimum threshold required to initiate this type of claim. Rather, clients or patients can claim to get an apology or explanation only. The procedure is easily initiated by sending a notification to the regulatory body, and the client or patient does not run the risk of bearing the costs of the procedure. The regulatory body can then decide to take actions itself or refer the claim to other authorities, including the Office of the Health Services Commissioner, the Office of the Privacy Commissioner or relevant registration bodies. In its authority to assess professional performance and fitness to practice, the regulatory body can consider the individual behaviour of a professional and draw conclusions as to whether it badly reflects on the profession. Thus, the scope of powers is broad and the consequences can be severe. The regulatory scheme is, however, subject to fundamental review.

Key Points

- The law of contracts protects the contractual relationship between parties, such as the one between psychiatrists or psychologists and their clients or patients.

- The law of torts protects the nature of certain relationships of trust, such as the one between psychiatrists or psychologists and their clients or patients.

- The law of equity protects the nature of confidential information, such as confidential information obtained in mental health services.

- When a breach of confidentiality is claimed, it is usually the client or patient who bears the burden of proof. Proof in civil claims is assessed on a balance of probabilities.

- Breaches of confidentiality claims consider such terms as what can be 'reasonably expected' or what is 'reasonable care and skill'. These terms are open to interpretation.

- The common law has not yet developed clear and comprehensive guidance on how to interpret these elements.

- Breaches in confidentiality do not typically result in measurable injury or loss.

CHAPTER 5

Common Law Exceptions and Limitations to Maintaining Confidentiality

The previous chapter focused on laws relating to the protection of confidential information. Although the law recognises that there is a general duty on health professionals to maintain confidentiality, this protection is subject to exceptions and limitations. This chapter outlines the ways in which exceptions and limitations to confidentiality have evolved through the common law (judge-made law). Chapter Six will then provide an overview of some of the statutory provisions relating to the disclosure of confidential information.

The common law develops on a case-by-case basis, and it has not yet provided a definitive and comprehensive ruling on the boundaries of confidentiality. However, it does provide some indication of the circumstances in which mental health professionals can disclose confidential information. In its review of common law developments, this chapter briefly outlines a number of relevant cases. It will refer specifically to judicial statements in which judges have considered the criteria for deciding whether an individual is permitted or compelled to disclose information.

First, this chapter explains how, contrary to what many mental health professionals believe, in Australia there is not yet a common law *duty* to disclose confidential information. The chapter then outlines the circumstances in which mental health professionals have been *permitted* to disclose confidential information (discretion to disclose).

The Absence of a Common Law Duty to Disclose

In Australia the common law has not yet imposed a duty to disclose information in circumstances where an individual is thought to be at risk of harming others. While there has been much discussion in North America about 'a duty to warn' third parties potentially at risk of harm, there has not been a case in Australia that has given rise to such a duty. The relevant case law in Australia is concerned with a *discretion* to disclose confidential information rather than a *duty* to do so (Kämpf, McSherry, Thomas, & Abrahams, 2008) and this is discussed in the section entitled 'The Common Law in Australia' in this chapter.

The question as to whether there is a duty to warn or to protect third parties has been much debated in the United States of America, particularly after the famous Californian case of *Tarasoff v Regents of the University of California* 17 Cal 3d 425 (1976), a decision that has also been discussed in the Australian context (Hands, 1999; Knowles & McMahon, 1995; Koocher, 1995; McMahon, 1992; McMahon, 2006; McSherry, 2001; Mendelson & Mendelson, 1991; Michalowski, 2003).

The *Tarasoff* case involved a situation in which a student, Prosenjit Poddar, told a psychologist who worked at a university student health centre that he would kill an unnamed girl (who was readily identifiable as Tatiana Tarasoff) when she returned home from spending the summer in Brazil. The psychologist contacted the campus police, stating that Poddar should be committed to a mental health facility and also sent a letter to the police chief requesting the assistance of the police department in securing Poddar's confinement. The police initially took the student into custody, but released him shortly afterwards. Several weeks later, he killed Tatiana Tarasoff.

In a civil action brought by the parents of Tatiana Tarasoff, the questions arose as to (1) whether the psychologist had a legal duty to warn the potential victim, or her parents, in order to protect her, and (2) whether, if such a duty existed, the psychologist had breached that duty. The Supreme Court of California held that a duty to use reasonable care to protect an identifiable victim from being killed existed and overrode therapeutic confidentiality.

Although this case has not been uniformly followed in the United States of America, and has declined in legal significance due to the enactment of legislation limiting its scope (McSherry, 2001; Walcott, Cerundolo, & Beck, 2001), it initially considerably broadened mental health professionals' scope for liability.

While the Californian case of *Tarasoff v Regents of the University of California* 17 Cal 3d 425 (1976) was the first case to establish a duty to warn an identifiable victim of potential harm, it is important to note that the Canadian, English and New Zealand courts have shied away from establishing a 'duty to protect' (McSherry, 2001). The focus instead has been on justifications for breaching confidentiality, which is discussed in the next section.

Key Points

- *Tarasoff's* case established a duty to warn an identifiable victim of potential harm in California, but this has declined in legal significance.
- *Tarasoff's* case does not apply to mental health professionals in Australia.

Common Law Discretion to Disclose

The common law in Canada, England and New Zealand has gradually clarified in which circumstances mental health professionals are permitted to disclose confidential information. This section outlines the main cases in these countries, while the next section sets out the relevant common law in Australia.

The Common Law in Canada

The main case dealing with disclosure of confidential information in Canada is that of *Smith v Jones* (1999) 132 CCC (3d) 239. This case concerned a man, 'Jones', who was charged with aggravated sexual assault on a prostitute. His counsel referred him to a psychiatrist, 'Dr Smith', for the purpose of preparing a defence or writing a submission for sentencing in the event of a guilty plea. During the interview, Jones told Dr Smith that he deliberately chose a small woman as his first victim because she could be readily overwhelmed and that he planned her assault as a trial to rape, kidnap and kill more prostitutes. Dr Smith telephoned Jones' counsel and said that in his opinion, Jones was at risk of committing future offences unless he received treatment. When Dr Smith later discovered from Jones' counsel that he would not be called to give evidence, he sought a declaration that he was entitled to disclose the information that he had in his possession in the interests of public safety.

The question that subsequently came before the Canadian courts was whether Dr Smith was entitled to disclose the confidential information to the prosecution and to the police. A majority of six judges of the Supreme Court of Canada (with three dissenting) held that solicitor–client privilege *may* be set aside when there is a danger to public safety and death or serious bodily harm is imminent.

In delivering the majority judgement, Cory J identified three criteria that need to be considered when deciding whether confidentiality can be breached in the interests of public safety. He stated that (at 249):

- There needs to be a clear risk to an identifiable person or group of persons;
- The risk must be one of serious bodily or psychological harm or death; and
- The risk must be imminent.

For the assessment of imminence, Cory J stated:

> The nature of threat must be such that it creates a sense of urgency. This sense of urgency may be applicable to some time in the future. Depending on the seriousness and clarity of the threat, it will not always be necessary to impose a particular time limit on the risk. It is sufficient if there is a clear and imminent threat of serious bodily harm to an identifiable group, and if this threat is made in such a manner that a sense of urgency is created. (at 251)

While this case deals specifically with the issue of solicitor–client privilege and it does not have to be followed in Australia, the three-step test set out by Cory J provides some guidance to mental health professionals in assessing when to breach confidentiality in the public interest (see further McSherry, 2001).

The Common Law in England

In England, the leading case on breaching confidentiality is that of *W v Egdell* [1990] 1 All ER 835, which focuses on the circumstances in which mental health professionals are permitted, but not compelled, to disclose confidential information. In this case, the plaintiff, 'W', sued a psychiatrist, Dr Egdell, for damages for breach of confidence.

W, who had been diagnosed as having paranoid schizophrenia, was detained without limit in a secure hospital after he killed five people and injured two others. Twelve years later, W applied for a transfer to a regional secure unit. W's solicitors sought a report from Dr Egdell for the purposes of a forthcoming hearing before the Mental Health Review Tribunal. Dr Egdell's report concluded that W had a 'seriously abnormal interest in the making of home made bombs' and stated that W should not be transferred to a regional secure unit. On the basis of this report, W, through his solicitors, withdrew his application. Dr Egdell asked W's solicitors to disclose his report to the Assistant Medical Director of the secure unit. When the solicitors declined to do so, he sent a copy of his report to the Assistant Medical Director and subsequently to the Home Office.

When W's case was later referred to the Mental Health Review Tribunal, W became aware of what Dr Egdell had done. He issued writs claiming injunctions to restrain further disclosure and delivery of all copies of the report as well as damages for breach of confidence. W's application and a subsequent appeal, however, were dismissed.

The Court of Appeal confirmed that the Dr Egdell had a duty of confidence, but held that it was outweighed by competing public interests. Lord Justice Bingham stated that:

> the law recognises an important public interest in
> maintaining professional duties of confidence, but ...
> the law treats such duties not as absolute but as liable
> to be overridden where there is held to be a stronger
> public interest in disclosure. (at 849)

He referred to examples such as a public interest in the administration of justice (at 847), in complying with the law (at 847), or in reducing or eliminating a risk to public safety (at 846). When balancing the competing public interests, Bingham J stated:

> [A] restricted patient who believes himself unnecessarily confined has, of all members of society, perhaps the greatest need for a professional advisor who is truly independent and reliably discreet ... Only the most compelling circumstances could justify a doctor in acting in a way which would injure the immediate interests of his patient. (at 852)

Giving consideration to the severity of W's past crimes (the number and nature of his killings) and the severity of his mental illness, Bingham J balanced the public interest in maintaining therapeutic confidence against the public interest in protecting others against possible violence. He found that the public interest in protecting others prevailed. To reach this decision it was, however, important that the information in the psychiatrist's report was relevant and that its release was restricted to the proper authorities.

In the same decision, Brown J clarified that in order to justify the premise that disclosing confidential information served to reduce or eliminate a risk to public safety, four elements must be shown (at 846):

- The risk to public safety must be real, immediate and serious;
- The risk must be substantially reduced by the disclosure;
- The disclosure may not be greater than is reasonably necessary to minimise the risk; and
- The consequent damage to the public interest protected by the duty of confidence must be outweighed by the public interest in minimising the risk.

Whether there is a duty to warn is closely related to the question of a duty of care and the degree to which such a duty of care might apply. The case of *Clunis v Camden and Islington Health Authority* [1998] 3 All ER 180 concerned a man who had a history of mental disorder and seriously violent behaviour. Approximately four weeks after his discharge from hospital, he stabbed a man to death. The court found that the question of whether there is a common law duty of care is 'profoundly influenced by the surrounding statutory framework' (at 192, further references omitted).

The statutory framework is 'a major consideration in deciding whether it is fair and reasonable for the local health authority to be held responsible for errors and omissions of the kind alleged' (at 192). However, even though the relevant mental health legislation provided for after-care following discharge and allowed for detention, if it is necessary in the interests of the patient or for the protection of other persons, the court doubted that Parliament intended to impose liability on health professions which give rise to a claim for damages (at 192 and 193).

This indicates that the common law in England is hesitant to endorse a duty on health professionals to exercise powers with the consequence of liability. This applies in particular when statutory law gives health professionals discretion as to whether or not to disclose confidential information. When it comes to deciding whether to disclose confidential information the common law has set up a range of criteria for mental health professionals to balance conflicting interests based on a case-by-case assessment.

The Common Law in New Zealand

There are a number of cases in New Zealand that deal with disclosure of confidential information in a health context. Most of these deal with disclosure in the forensic arena. However, the New Zealand High Court decision in *Duncan v Medical Practitioners Disciplinary Committee* [1986] 1 NZLR 513 is slightly different in dealing with an appeal in relation to disciplinary proceedings against a medical practitioner. Dr Duncan told the local police and a bus passenger that one of his patients, a bus driver, was medically unfit to drive and should have his licence revoked. The bus driver made a complaint to the Medical Practitioners Disciplinary Committee against Dr Duncan for a breach of patient confidentiality. The complaint led to a finding of professional misconduct.

Instead of appealing to the Medical Council, Dr Duncan made allegations to the media. A Preliminary Proceedings Committee heard further complaints against Dr Duncan and this Committee formulated a charge of disgraceful conduct for an inquiry by the

Medical Council. Dr Duncan challenged the validity of the charge and initiated a proceedings for judicial review.

Justice Jeffries dismissed this application for review. He held that confidential information should only be disclosed in exceptional circumstances such as when there is an immediate danger to another person's life and urgent action is required (at 521). He further stated that confidentiality is not breached if health care providers consult with colleagues on the treatment of their patient, if they use common filing systems or if the information is used for some statistical, accounting, data processing or other legitimate purpose (at 521). Justice Jeffries also stated that doctors may reveal confidential information if they need to defend themselves or others against accusations of wrongful conduct (at 521). In the case of disclosure to lay persons, he stated that disclosure of confidential information must be confined to 'exceptional circumstances, and then only if the public interest was paramount' (at 521). Disclosure should rather be targeted to responsible authorities. He explained:

> There may be occasions, they are fortunately rare, when a doctor receives information involving a patient that another's life is immediately endangered and urgent action is required. The doctor must then exercise his professional judgement based upon the circumstances, and if he fairly and reasonably believes such a danger exists then he must act unhesitatingly to prevent injury or loss of life even if there is to be a breach of confidentiality. If his actions later are to be scrutinised as to their correctness, he can be confident any official inquiry will be by people sympathetic about the predicament he faced. (at 521)

On the facts, Justice Jeffries held that the Disciplinary Committee had been correct in finding that there had not been exceptional circumstances such as to breach confidentiality.

In the subsequent case of *Van de Wetering and Others v Capital Coast Health Limited* (unreported, High Court of New Zealand, Wellington Registry, 19 May 2000), Master Thomson signalled a cautious approach to circumstances somewhat similar to *Tarasoff's* case when he struck out a number of claims in negligence for the breach of a common law and statutory duty of care. This case involved a man under psychiatric care who killed four people and wounded another. The question arose as to whether the treating psychiatrist knew or ought to have known how dangerous his patient was and whether he had a duty to protect the public from this patient. Ultimately, Thomson J did not impose such a duty of care, stating that it would create 'liability in an indeterminate amount for an indeterminate time to an indeterminate class' (at 10). He elaborated that:

> A responsible clinician has to be able to focus exclusively on the best interests of the patient. It would impose an intolerable burden on a clinician to be under the constant threat or legal responsibility for the conduct of his/her patient. Otherwise, and plainly contrary to public policy, the clinician will inevitably sublimate or deprioritise the patient's best interests in favour of cautious self-protection. (at 16)

In *Maulolo v Hutt Valley Health Corporation Ltd* [2002] NZAR 375, 'P' killed his girlfriend, Fiona Maulolo, approximately a year after P had been released from compulsory treatment as a psychiatric patient. P was subsequently found not guilty of murder on the ground of insanity. An action for negligence was brought against the hospital by the relatives of the victim on the basis that P should not have been released into the community. The plaintiff's statement of claim was struck out by Master Thomson and this decision was affirmed in a review by Justice Wild of the High Court. The latter held that there was no duty of care owed by the hospital to the relatives of the deceased victim because there was not a sufficiently proximate relationship between the defendant hospital and the plaintiffs.

Policy considerations played a role in the decision not to find a duty of care owed by the hospital in that it would be against the public interest to find such a duty. Justice Wild (at 382) found that the policy considerations were similar to those raised in *Van de Wetering* and that it had been open to the Master to 'take the view that the imposition of duties here would not be in the public interest' (at 384).

The subsequent case of *Ellis v Counties Manukau District Health Board* [2007] 1 NZLR 196 concerned Paul Ellis who killed his father two weeks after his release from compulsory treatment. Ellis sued the Health Board on the basis that it had been negligent in failing to properly assess, treat and detain him in order to prevent harm to others. In an application by the Board to strike out the statement of claim, Justice Potter undertook an extensive analysis of whether a psychiatrist has a common law duty to take reasonable care to detain certain individuals to prevent them from causing harm to themselves or others. Justice Potter granted the application that the Statement of Claim be struck out, stating that some features of mental health legislation point away from finding a duty of care. Justice Potter (at 228) pointed in particular to the fact that the *Mental Health (Compulsory Assessment and Treatment) Act 1992* (NZ):

- focuses on providing assessment and treatment in the least restrictive environment;
- does not impose a duty on the responsible clinician to detain a patient;
- does not permit the responsible clinician to detain a patient indefinitely;
- enables the judicial review of the responsible clinician's power or discretion to detain; and
- does not impose a duty on the responsible clinician to 'resection' a patient.

Justice Potter also stated that protecting the rights of those with mental illnesses is a factor going against imposing a duty to detain upon mental health professionals:

> Mentally unwell persons, their vulnerability, their safety and that of the community, are the interests and concerns which the [NZ] Act seeks to balance. But mentally disordered persons, who for that very reason are vulnerable, have rights that require protection. Those rights require that care is taken in detaining patients, as much as in treating and releasing them. In my view, vulnerability cannot, and does not under the Act, give rise to a duty to detain, imposed upon the responsible clinician or other health professional. (at 168)

Although this decision focused on whether or not there should be a duty to detain placed on mental health professionals and not a duty to warn, it shows that courts are hesitant to endorse mental health professionals' liability for a patient's actions.

Key Points

- Canadian, English and New Zealand courts have shied away from establishing a 'duty to protect'.
- The cases in these countries emphasise that disclosure of confidential information should be exceptional in nature.
- In weighing up whether to disclose confidential information, the courts have looked at whether:
  - there is a clear risk to an identifiable person or group of persons;
  - there is an imminent risk of serious bodily or psychological harm or death; and
  - the public interest protected by the duty of confidence is outweighed by the public interest in minimising the risk of harm.

The Common Law in Australia

Australian law currently does not impose a duty to disclose confidential information in *Tarasoff*-like situations. It seems that if a similar case arises in Australia, following the approach taken in Canada, England and New Zealand, the courts will set out when health professionals are permitted to disclose confidential information, rather than develop a legal duty to protect (McSherry, 2001, p. 18).

The case of *R v Lowe* [1997] 2 VR 465 focused on whether confidential information was admissible as evidence. However, the Court of Appeal of the Supreme Court of Victoria extended its discussion to whether there is a duty to disclose confidential information concerning persons who are thought to pose a risk of harming others. The Court of Appeal unanimously held that 'the private confidence of health service providers is subordinated to the wider public interest where disclosure will aid the protection of the public from a specific and identifiable threat' (at 466). It stated that common law and statute law clearly allow disclosure in the public interest, 'at least when it comes to disclosing information in the interests of prosecuting serious crime and/or protecting public safety' (at 485). However, the Court of Appeal supported the idea that courts should be 'slow to admit evidence of a confessional nature which is obtained in trust and confidence by a therapist from her patient' (at 485). While the Court of Appeal stated that there is 'an emerging view that a duty of disclosure exists' (at 485), this is not a definitive statement that is binding on other courts as the issue was not crucial in deciding the case.

In *Kadian v Richards* (2004) 61 NSWLR 222 (affirmed by *Richards v Kadian* (2005) 64 NSWLR 204), a case that concerned the question of whether patients could waive a right of confidentiality, Justice Campbell of the Supreme Court of New South Wales also addressed a doctor's obligation of confidence. Justice Campbell re-confirmed the position in *Hunter v Mann* [1974] QB 767 at 772 that '[a] doctor is under a duty not to voluntarily disclose, without the consent of his or her patient, information which the doctor has gained in his or her professional capacity save in very exceptional circumstances' (at para. [44]). Justice Campbell went on to state that:

> Those 'very exceptional' circumstances include circumstances where the information which the doctor obtains is information which, if not disclosed, could endanger the lives or health of others, where the information which the doctor gains in the relationship is information concerning a dishonesty or other 'iniquity' inherently incapable of being the subject matter of an obligation of confidence, where the information is acquired in the course of an actual or reasonably apprehended breach of the criminal law or where statute requires certain types of information to be disclosed. (at [45], further references omitted)

President Maxwell of the Court of Appeal of the Supreme Court of Victoria also confirmed in the *Royal Women's Hospital v Medical Practitioners Board of Victoria* (2006) 15 VR 22 at 58 that the 'importance of maintaining the confidentiality of the patient–doctor relationship ... is a matter of high public importance ... [and] of concern to the whole community'.

As is the case in New Zealand, recent Australian case law indicates that courts will be cautious about endorsing any duty of care on mental health professionals to protect third parties from harm. The decisions in *Presland v Hunter Area Health Service* [2003] NSWSC 754 and *Hunter Area Health Service v Presland* (2005) 63 NSWLR 22 concerned a plaintiff, Kevin Presland, suing his treating psychiatrist and the employing health service for failing to detain him, and thus failing to prevent him from killing his brother's fiancée while he was affected by psychosis.

Justice Adams in the New South Wales Supreme Court decisions in *Presland v Hunter Area Health Service* [2003] NSWSC 754 found the psychiatrist, and vicariously the Hunter Area Health Service, negligent in failing to detain Presland, and thus responsible for the adverse outcomes suffered by Presland including his incarceration in a mental institution following a plea of not guilty on the grounds of mental impairment. This decision gave rise to discussion as to what this would mean for psychiatric inpatient services (Freckelton, 2003; Scott, 2006).

The defendants appealed and in a two-to-one decision in the New South Wales Court of Appeal (Sheller JA and Santow JA, Spigelman CJ dissenting) the initial decision by Justice Adams was overturned on policy grounds. The reasoning of the majority in the Court of Appeal was that although negligence could be established against the appellants, it was considered inappropriate for Presland to be awarded damages after killing another person.

The High Court in *Stuart v Kirkland-Veenstra* (2009) 237 CLR 215 also shows a reluctance to impose any duty of care on third parties. Tania Kirkland-Veenstra sued two police officers for negligently failing to prevent her husband's suicide, which she claimed subsequently caused her psychiatric injury. The majority of the Victorian Court of Appeal in *Kirkland-Veenstra v Stuart* (2008) Aust Torts Reports ¶81–936 held that in addition to owing the deceased, Ronald Veenstra, a duty of care to prevent his suicide, the police officers also owed Tania Kirkland-Veenstra a duty of care in relation to her mental health.

On appeal, this majority decision was unanimously overturned by the High Court. In three separate judgements, the justices of the

High Court held that the police officers did not owe Ronald Veenstra a duty of care to prevent him from committing suicide in the circumstances and there was therefore no duty of care owed to Tania Kirkland-Veenstra. The Court made this decision upon very narrow grounds and therefore broader questions in relation to the imposition of duties of care have not been resolved.

In his dissenting judgment in *Hunter Area Health Service v Presland* (2005) 63 NSWLR 22 at 27, Spigelman CJ set out four criteria for establishing a common law duty of care to a third party:

- inquiry into the purpose of the statute in relation to the relevant risk;
- control by the mental health professional over the relevant risk;
- the vulnerability of the victim to the relevant risk; and
- the coherence of imposing such a duty in the statutory context.

This analysis may prove a starting point for future cases dealing with the disclosure of confidential information on the basis of harm to others.

Rangarajan and McSherry (2009) argue that it is unlikely that a 'duty to detain' will be imposed in Australia because there are strong policy reasons why this should not be the case, such as:

- over-cautious practice resulting in a decreased threshold to continue to detain psychiatric patients;
- failing to comply with the requirement of 'least restrictive' treatment as framed mental health legislation; and
- onerous resource implications.

Similar reasoning would seem to imply that a 'duty to protect' will not be imposed, but Australian law will follow the lead of Canada, England and New Zealand in emphasising that disclosure of confidential information should be exceptional in nature.

Key Points

- Australian courts have not established a 'duty to protect' or a 'duty to warn' third parties and it seems unlikely that such a duty will be imposed.
- Australian courts have emphasised the importance of confidentiality in therapeutic relationships as a matter of public and private interests.
- The Australian cases indicate that disclosure of confidential information should be exceptional in nature.
- Disclosure of confidential information is permitted, if:
  - legislation allows disclosure;
  - disclosure serves matters of high public importance, such as prosecuting serious crimes, protecting public health and safety, and preventing danger to the life or health of the client or patient or others.

Conclusion

The cases outlined in this chapter indicate that the common law generally protects confidentiality in therapeutic settings. The common law develops on a case-by-case basis and, in Australia, there has not yet been a comprehensive ruling on the boundaries of confidentiality in cases that do not involve serious crimes or court proceedings.

However, when looking at the circumstances in which judges have allowed the disclosure of confidential information, many of the underlying reasons come down to protecting public interests that compete with but override the public interest in protecting confidentiality. Some of the more recent decisions explicitly balance competing public interests, indicating that this will become an increasingly important exercise.

The courts in Canada, England, New Zealand and Australia have shied away from imposing a duty on mental health professionals to disclose information, particularly if it would run the risk of impeding the balancing exercise. Mental health professionals must therefore base any decision to disclose information on their professional judgement, a careful balance of competing interests, and general ethical and legal principles.

CHAPTER 6

Statutory Schemes

One of the most complex aspects of the law on confidentiality is trying to understand the variety of legislative provisions dealing with confidential information and its interplay with the common law. It is important to differentiate between the statutory schemes within Commonwealth legislation and the states' and territories' legislation that relate to private or confidential information.

Confidentiality provisions and provisions for the disclosure of certain information can be found in legislation relating to mental health care; court proceedings; criminal investigations; the use, collection and storage of health information; guardianship; and other areas. The following broad overview of legislative requirements will focus on provisions that specifically address health information or provisions that are particularly relevant to mental health care settings. The overview will include a list of some of the relevant provisions on matters of confidentiality within federal, state and territory legislation. Although this list is not exhaustive, it provides a reference point for understanding the scope of current provisions. If there is some doubt as to which statutory provisions apply to a practical dilemma, it is important and helpful to seek professional advice from indemnity insurers and legal counsel to assist in decision-making.

Privacy and Health Records Legislation

The *Privacy Act 1988* (Cth) evolved in response to international law developments concerning the protection of privacy. In particular, privacy issues are addressed in:

- the United Nations International Covenant on Civil and Political Rights (ICCPR) (http://www2.ohchr.org/english/law/ccpr.htm);
- the Organisation for Economic Co-operation and Development (OECD) Privacy Guidelines (available at http://www.oecd.org/); and
- the Council of Europe's Convention for the Protection of Individuals with Regard to Automatic Processing of Personal Data (http://epic.org/privacy/intl/coeconvention/).

An investigation into Australia's privacy protection scheme suggested that improvements were necessary in order to comply with international standards (Law Reform Commission, 1983). In response to that finding, privacy legislation was enacted.

The *Privacy Act 1988* (Cth) establishes a legal obligation for employees to keep health records confidential. It also distinguishes between two sets of principles: the Information Privacy Principles (IPP) and the National Privacy Principles (NPP). The IPP apply to federal and Australian Capital Territory government agencies, while the NPP apply to parts of the private sector and individuals. The fact that the *Privacy Act* establishes these two distinctive schemes to handle health information in the private and public sectors can be confusing and has attracted criticism (Office of the Privacy Commissioner, 2005, 64ff).

As the NPP provide specific rules to protect sensitive health information, this type of information is subject to stronger protection than other private information. Principle 2 of the NPP generally prohibits disclosure of personal health information beyond its primary purpose. The primary purpose is typically the diagnosis and treatment of the client or patient. But disclosure is permissible in the following circumstances:

- if it is directly related to the primary purpose and within the client's or patient's reasonable expectations;
- if the client or patient consents to it; or
- if disclosure is required or authorised by law.

Sensitive health information may also be disclosed in order to lessen or prevent either a serious and imminent threat to an individual's life, health or safety, or a serious threat to public health or safety. It should be noted, however, that the NPP do not impose a duty to disclose information. Note 2 in the NPP Schedule 3.2.1 explicitly states that 'an organisation is always entitled not to disclose personal information in the absence of a legal obligation to disclose it'.

All states and territories have also enacted specific health records and information privacy legislation. Table 6.1 sets out the main provisions in this area. The provisions in these statutes are generally more detailed than those included in mental health legislation. They are mostly based on the IPP or NPP, found in the *Privacy Act 1988* (Cth). In turn, they also distinguish between the public and private service sectors and, depending on whether a mental health service is part of the public or private sector, different statutes apply in some states and territories. As the health record provisions are similar to the IPP and NPP of the *Privacy Act 1988* (Cth), further elaboration will be omitted.

However, it is worth noting that all relevant provisions permit disclosure in an emergency situation when that disclosure is necessary to lessen or prevent a serious and imminent threat to the life, health or safety of a person. Confidential information may also be disclosed to lessen or prevent a serious threat to public health or public safety.

Key Points

- The Privacy Act 1988 (Cth) and health records statutes protect health records and information from disclosure.
- Exceptions to the general rule of confidentiality permit disclosure in the following circumstances:
  - if disclosing confidential information is directly related to the treatment of the client or patient or within that client's or patient's reasonable expectations
  - if the client or patient consents to disclosing confidential information;
  - if disclosure serves to lessen or prevent either a serious and imminent threat to an individual's life, health or safety, or a serious threat to public health or safety;
  - if disclosure is otherwise authorised by law.

Table 6.1
Most Relevant Legislation on Disclosure of Health Information

Jurisdiction	Sector	Legislation
ACT	Public	*Health Records (Privacy and Access) Act 1997* (ACT), Privacy Principle 10
	Private	*Health Records (Privacy and Access) Act 1997* (ACT), Privacy Principle 10
NSW	Public	*Health Records and Information Privacy Act 2002* (NSW), Health Privacy Principle 10
	Private	*Health Records and Information Privacy Act 2002* (NSW), Health Privacy Principle 10
NT	Public	*Information Act 2006* (NT), section 148, Information Privacy Principle 2
	Private	*Privacy Act 1988* (Cth), National Privacy Principle 2
Qld	Public	Information Standard 42 — Information Privacy*
		Information Standard 42A — Information Privacy for the Queensland Department of Health*
	Private	*Privacy Act 1988* (Cth), National Privacy Principle 2
SA	Public	Information Privacy Principles Instruction PC012 1992*
	Private	*Privacy Act 1988* (Cth), National Privacy Principle 2
Tas	Public	*Personal Information Protection Act 2004* (Tas), Personal Information Privacy Principle 2
	Private	*Privacy Act 1988* (Cth), National Privacy Principle 2
Vic	Public	*Health Records Act 2001* (Vic), National Privacy Principle 2
	Private	*Health Records Act 2001* (Vic), Health Privacy Principle 2
WA	Public	Information Privacy Bill 2007 (WA), section 131, Information Privacy Principle 2 (now lapsed)
	Private	Information Privacy Bill 2007 (WA), section 131, National Privacy Principle 2 (now lapsed)

Note: All legislation is referred to as it applied on 1 August 2009.

*Administrative scheme (legislative requirements may supersede).

Mental Health Legislation
General Provisions Dealing with Confidentiality

All Australian states and territories have specific mental health legislation in place. With the exception of the Australian Capital Territory, each piece of mental health legislation incorporates specific provisions that generally protect confidentiality in mental health settings. The *Mental Health (Treatment and Care) Act 1994* in the Australian Capital Territory is currently under review and it may be that a revised Act will contain confidentiality provisions.

The relevant mental health Acts in Australia use different formulations and define the scope and context of services differently. However, with the exception of the Australian Capital Territory, they essentially protect the information that a mental health professional obtains when he or she exercises functions or powers under the mental health legislation. If mental health professionals who fall under the application of the mental health legislation do not comply with these provisions, various penalties apply.

However, the relevant mental health Acts contain many exceptions and limitations to the duty to maintain confidentiality. As a general observation, it is worth noting that confidential information may be disclosed in the following situations or to the following individuals:

- with the client's consent;
- when the disclosure is required or authorised by the mental health legislation or other legal provisions;
- to nominated carers or guardians in certain circumstances;
- for the purpose of criminal investigations or criminal proceedings; and
- for statistical analysis and research purposes, provided that there is compliance with further requirements.

Table 6.2 sets out the main provisions in this area. The actual language of the relevant provisions has been used wherever possible, with some paraphrasing.

Table 6.2
Provisions Dealing with Confidentiality in Mental Health Legislation

Jurisdiction and name of Act	Statement on confidentiality	Disclosure with client's consent	Disclosure pursuant to other legislation	Disclosure to carers or guardians	Disclosure for criminal investigations or proceedings	Disclosure for research
NSW *Mental Health Act 2007*	A person must not disclose any information obtained in connection with the administration or execution of the Act (s 189(1))	A person may disclose information with the consent of the person from whom the information was obtained (s 189(1)(a))	In connection with the administration or execution of the *Mental Health (Forensic Provisions) Act 1990* (s 189(1(b))	To a primary carer of a person in connection with the provision of care or treatment to the person (s 189(1)(c))	For the purposes of any legal proceedings arising out of the Act (s 189(1)(d))	For a purpose referred to in health privacy principle 10(1)(f)(research) under the *Health Records and Information Privacy Act 2002*
QLD *Mental Health Act 2000*	Nobody may disclose the information, or give access to a document about another person's affairs, to anyone else (s 528(1)–(2)). Exceptions are provided for in certain circumstances (s 530).	If the person to whom the information relates agrees to the disclosure or giving of access and the person is an adult when the agreement is given (s 528(3)(d); s 529(3)(b))	May disclose if the disclosure or giving of access is otherwise required or permitted by law (s 528(3)(c); s 529(3)(a)) or necessary to perform the person's functions under the Act (s 528(3)(b))			

Table 6.2 (continued)
Provisions Dealing with Confidentiality in Mental Health Legislation

Jurisdiction and name of Act	Statement on confidentiality	Disclosure with client's consent	Disclosure pursuant to other legislation	Disclosure to carers or guardians	Disclosure for criminal investigations or proceedings	Disclosure for research
SA *Mental Health Act 2009*	A person engaged or formerly engaged in the administration of this Act must not disclose personal information relating to a person obtained in the course of administration of this Act except to the extent that he or she may be authorised or required to disclose that information by the Chief Executive (s 106(1))	May disclose information at the request, or with the consent, of the person to whom the information relates or a guardian or medical agent of the person (s 106(2)(b))	May disclose information as required by law, or as required for the administration of the Act or a law of another State or Territory of the Commonwealth (s 106(2)(a))	May disclose information to a relative, carer or friend of the person to whom the information relates if the disclosure is reasonably required for the treatment, care or rehabilitation of the person and there is no reason to believe that the disclosure would be contrary to the person's best interests (s 106(2)(c))	May disclose information if it is reasonably required to lessen or prevent a serious threat to the life, health or safety of a person, or a serious threat to public health or safety (s 106(2)(e))	May disclose information for medical or social research purposes if the research methodology has been approved by an ethics committee and there is no reason to believe that the disclosure would be contrary to the person's best interests (s 106(2)(f))

continued over

Table 6.2 (continued)
Provisions Dealing with Confidentiality in Mental Health Legislation

Jurisdiction and name of Act	Statement on confidentiality	Disclosure with client's consent	Disclosure pursuant to other legislation	Disclosure to carers or guardians	Disclosure for criminal investigations or proceedings	Disclosure for research
Tas *Mental Health Act 1996*	A person who obtains information of a person or confidential nature about a person in the exercise of powers or functions under this Act must not disclose the information except as provided for under the Act (s 90(1))	The information may be disclosed if the disclosure is authorised by the person to whom it relates (s 90(2)(a))	If the disclosure is reasonably required for the care or treatment of the person to whom the information relates or for the administration of the Act (s 90(2)(b))			
Vic *Mental Health Act 1986*	A relevant person must not, except to the extent necessary to carry out functions or exercise powers, give to (s 120A(3)(a))	May disclose if the person has given prior consent (either express or implied) (s 120A(3)(a))	May disclose information as described in the Health Privacy Principles in the Health Records Act 2001 (s 120A(3)(ea))	May disclose information to a guardian, family member or primary carer if the information is	May give information to a court in the course of criminal proceedings (s 120A(3)(b))	May disclose information to the Australian Statistician (s 120A(3)(f)) May disclose for the purposes of medical

Table 6.2 (continued)
Provisions Dealing with Confidentiality in Mental Health Legislation

Jurisdiction and name of Act	Statement on confidentiality	Disclosure with client's consent	Disclosure pursuant to other legislation	Disclosure to carers or guardians	Disclosure for criminal investigations or proceedings	Disclosure for research
Vic (continued) *Mental Health Act 1986*	any other person, whether directly or indirectly, any information acquired by reason of being a relevant person, if a person who is or has been a patient of, or has received psychiatric services from, a relevant psychiatric service could be identified from that information (s 120A(2))		May disclose information to or by a person or a person in a class of persons, designated under s 141(5) of the Health Services Act 1988 in the course of carrying out support functions designated under that provision (s 120A(3)(ga)) May disclose information required in connection with any proceedings before the Board, Tribunal or Panel (s 120A(3)(h)–(ha))	reasonably required for the ongoing care of the person and the person receiving the information will be involved in providing that care (s 120A(3)(ca))		or social research if the use to which the information will be put and the research methodology have been approved by an ethics committee of the relevant psychiatric service, and the giving of information does not conflict with any prescribed requirements, and the giving of information is in accordance with the Health Privacy Principles in the Health Records Act 2001 (s 120A(3)(g))

continued over

Table 6.2 (continued)
Provisions Dealing with Confidentiality in Mental Health Legislation

Jurisdiction and name of Act	Statement on confidentiality	Disclosure with client's consent	Disclosure pursuant to other legislation	Disclosure to carers or guardians	Disclosure for criminal investigations or proceedings	Disclosure for research
WA *Mental Health Act* 1996	A person must not directly or indirectly divulge any personal information obtained by reason of any function that person has, or at any time had, in the administration of the Act (s 206(1))	May divulge personal information with the consent of the person to whom the information relates (s 206(2)(d))	May divulge personal information in the course of duty (s 206(2)(a)), or under the Act or another law (s 206(2)(b)) —		May divulge information for the purposes of the investigation of any suspected offence or the conduct of proceedings against any person for an offence (s 206(2)(c)) —	

Note: All legislation is referred to as it applied on 1 August 2009.

Disclosure for the Protection of Others

Sub-sections 91(2)(f)–(h) of the *Mental Health and Related Services Act 2005* (NT) and sub-section 106(2)(e) of the *Mental Health Act 2009* (SA) are the only legislative provisions that deal specifically with the disclosure of confidential information for the purpose of warning authorities about a client or patient considered to be at risk of harming others.

Sub-section 106(2)(e) of the *Mental Health Act 2009* (SA) states that persons engaged in administering the Act 'may disclose information if it is reasonably required to lessen or prevent a serious threat to the life, health or safety of a person, or a serious threat to public health or safety'. It is important to note that this gives discretion to the relevant person; it is not a mandatory requirement.

The exceptions to confidentiality in the Northern Territory are more complex. Sub-sections 91(2)(f)–(h) *permit* (that is, it is not mandatory) disclosure of confidential information to police officers and the Commissioner of Police or persons specifically nominated by the Commissioner of Police. Confidential information may be disclosed to the Commissioner of Police if the mental health professional 'reasonably believes' that the client or patient 'may harm himself or herself or represents a danger to the general community' (ss 91(2)(g)).

Sub-section 91(2)(f) also permits a mental health professional to disclose confidential information to a police officer if:

  (i)   the person to whom the information relates is in
        a situation requiring immediate intervention; and
  (ii) the person:
        (A) is likely to cause serious harm to himself or
            herself or to someone else; or
        (B) represents a substantial danger to the general
            community; and
  (iii) the information is relevant to the safe resolution
        of the situation.

In addition, sub-section 91(2)(h) permits a mental health professional to disclose confidential information to a police officer when 'it is required to prevent or lessen a serious or imminent threat to the life or health of the person, another person or the general community'.

Although legislative provisions enabling disclosure in the public interest exist only in South Australia and the Northern Territory at present, the latter scheme presents a staged approach, which is useful to consider in decision-making. Under the Northern Territory scheme, the more serious the risk, the more flexibility is given to a mental health professional in deciding to whom he or she may disclose confidential information. The legislation differentiates between harm, serious harm, and a serious and imminent threat to a life or to the health of a person.

The other Australian jurisdictions, however, do not specify how to deal with the disclosure of confidential information in emergency situations.

Key Points
- Mental health Acts contain provisions protecting the confidentiality of information about individuals with mental illnesses.
- Mental health Acts contain provisions providing for exceptions to the general duty to maintain confidentiality.
- The *Mental Health and Related Services Act 2005* (NT) and the *Mental Health Act 2009* (SA) are the only statutes that deal specifically with the disclosure of confidential information for the purpose of warning authorities about a client or patient considered to be at risk of harming others.

Mandatory Reporting of Child Abuse

In addition to the mental health care and confidential information legislation, various other statutory provisions such as those in public health legislation may require the disclosure of confidential information. The most discussed issue in this regard is the mandatory reporting of child abuse.

In most Australian jurisdictions, certain professionals are under a duty to report cases of child abuse. Table 6.3 sets out the main provisions dealing with mandatory reporting. There are penalties for nondisclosure where the person concerned is mandated to disclose the information and fails to do so. As in Table 6.2, the actual language of the Act has been included wherever possible with some paraphrasing.

Table 6.3
Disclosure Mandated in Cases of Child Abuse

Jurisdiction and name of Act	Who must report child abuse	When disclosure is mandatory	Who to report to
ACT *Children and Young People Act 2008* Section 356	Doctors, dentists, nurses, midwives, police officers and teachers, school counsellors (and others involved in the care of children)	The professional believes on reasonable grounds that a child or young person has experienced, or is experiencing, sexual abuse or non-accidental physical injury	The Chief Executive of ACT Health
NSW *Children and Young Persons (Care and Protection) Act 1998* Section 27	(a) A person who in the course of his or her professional work or other paid employment delivers health care, welfare, education, children's services, residential services or law enforcement, wholly or partly, to children; and (b) A person who holds a management position in an organisation and whose duties include direct responsibility for, or direct supervision of, the provision of health care, welfare, education, children's services, residential services or law enforcement, wholly or partly, to children'	(a) The person has reasonable grounds to suspect that a child is at risk of harm, and (b) Those grounds arise during the course of or from the person's work	The Director-General of the Department of Community Services

continued over

Table 6.3 (continued)
Disclosure Mandated in Cases of Child Abuse

Jurisdiction and name of Act	Who must report child abuse	When disclosure is mandatory	Who to report to
NT *Care and Protection of Children Act 2007* Section 26	Any person	The person believes, on reasonable grounds, that a child has been or is likely to be a victim of a sexual offence or otherwise has suffered or is likely to suffer harm or exploitation	The Chief Executive Officer of the Department of Health and Families A police officer
Qld *Public Health Act 2005* Section 191	Doctor or registered nurse	The doctor or nurse becomes aware, or reasonably suspects, during the practice of his or her profession that a child has been, is being or is likely to be harmed	The Chief Executive of the Department of Communities (Child Safety)
SA *Children's Protection Act 2003* Section 11	Medical practitioners, pharmacists, nurses, dentists, psychologists, police officers, community corrections officers, social workers, teachers, ministers of religion (and certain others involved in the care of children)	a) The relevant person suspects on reasonable grounds that a child has been or is being abused or neglected; and (b) the suspicion is formed in the course of the person's work (whether paid or voluntary) or of carrying out official duties	The Department of Education and Children's Services

Table 6.3 (continued)
Disclosure Mandated in Cases of Child Abuse

Jurisdiction and name of Act	Who must report child abuse	When disclosure is mandatory	Who to report to
Tas *Children, Young Persons and Their Families Act 1997* Section 14	Medical practitioners, nurses, dentists, psychologists, police officers, probation officers, teachers, child care workers	The prescribed person believes, suspects or knows, on reasonable grounds, that a child has been or is being abused or neglected or that there is a reasonable likelihood of a child being killed or abused or neglected by a person with whom the child resides	The Secretary of the Department of Health and Human Services
Vic *Children, Youth and Families Act 2005* Section 184	Medical practitioners, nurses, teachers, school principals, members of the police force	The relevant person forms the belief on reasonable grounds that a child is in need of protection on the basis that the child has suffered, or is likely to suffer, significant harm as a result of physical injury and the child's parents have not protected, or are unlikely to protect, the child from harm of that type, or the child has suffered, or is likely to suffer, significant harm as a result of sexual abuse and the child's parents have not protected, or are unlikely to protect, the child from harm of that type	The Secretary to the Department of Human Services

continued over

Table 6.3 (continued)
Disclosure Mandated in Cases of Child Abuse

Jurisdiction and name of Act	Who must report child abuse	When disclosure is mandatory	Who to report to
WA *Children and Community Services Act 2004* Section 124B	Doctors, nurses, midwives, police officers, teachers	The relevant person believes on reasonable grounds that a child has been the subject of sexual abuse or is the subject of ongoing sexual abuse and forms the belief in the course of the person's work	The Chief Executive Officer of the Department for Child Protection or a person approved by the Chief Executive Officer

Note: All legislation is referred to as it applied on 1 August 2009.

It should be noted that these statutes also contain provisions *permitting* disclosure by any person primarily on the basis of a reasonable belief that the child is being sexually or physically abused and some statutes include provisions protecting those who have disclosed information from legal liability. For example, while the *Child Protection Act 1999* (Qld) does not have mandatory reporting provisions, section 22 of that Act protects individuals from liability for the notification of, or information given to, the Chief Executive of the Department of Communities about alleged harm or risk of harm.

Many of the state and territory departments responsible for the care and protection of children have the requisite forms for reporting child abuse available on their websites.

Key Points

- All Australian jurisdictions now have statutory provisions relating to the mandatory reporting of child abuse by certain professionals.
- Disclosure of child abuse is also permitted by any person in certain circumstances.

Other Legislation

There are other statutes requiring the disclosure of confidential information particularly in relation to court proceedings. Each Australian jurisdiction has an *Evidence Act* that contains provisions enabling courts to request or compel a person to give evidence or produce documents and other statutes enable the issuing of subpoenas or summons to give evidence. Again, it is important to obtain legal advice if a court has issued documents requiring evidence in court or the disclosure of certain documents because there may be circumstances when such legal requests can be challenged.

When dealing with confidential information, the growing importance of human rights should also be considered. On a federal level, Australia does not have a bill or charter of rights, although discussion is now taking place about whether it is necessary to have one. The Australian Capital Territory and Victoria have legislative schemes in place, which provide limited protection of certain human rights (*Human Rights Act 2004* (ACT); *Charter of Human Rights and Responsibilities Act 2006* (Vic)).

The impact of these schemes is limited in that the human rights they enshrine are not legally enforceable and any laws that conflict with human rights standards cannot be struck down by the courts. Nevertheless, they serve as a reference point for judges in interpreting the law and as an indicator of the human rights commitment of the state or territory government that enacted the legislation. Beyond this, the human rights legislation has an important symbolic value and potential for the interpretation and application of human rights within the Australian legal framework. Thus, the *Human Rights Act 2004* (ACT) and the Victorian *Charter of Human Rights and Responsibilities* are relevant for guiding law and policy-making as well as individual decision-making when applying the law.

An individual's right to privacy is discussed in section 12 of the *Human Rights Act 2004* (ACT) and Part 2 of the Victorian *Charter of Human Rights and Responsibilities*. The concept of privacy derives from the protection of autonomy and the individual freedom to choose with whom to share private information. It is a concept that is protected in international human rights documents and it is expected that it will increasingly influence law reform and the development of the common law in Australia. With Australia also having ratified the United Nations *Convention on the Rights of Persons with Disabilities* in July 2008, Australia has strengthened its human rights commitment in particular in the mental health area.

Key Points

- Confidentiality provisions and provisions for the disclosure of certain information can be found in many different statutes.
- Some of the most important provisions can be found in privacy and health records legislation, mental health Acts and legislation dealing with the mandatory disclosure of information regarding child abuse.
- The concept of privacy is protected in international human rights documents, and statutory exceptions are generally carefully circumscribed.
- Australian legislation mandates breaching confidentiality only in limited, clearly identified situations, such as mandatory reporting of child abuse.

CHAPTER 7

Ethical Decision-Making
in Confidentiality Dilemmas

> Lack of awareness or misunderstanding of an ethical
> standard is not itself a defence to an allegation of
> unethical conduct.
> (Australian Psychological Society, Code of Ethics, p. 10)

As any mental health professional knows, it is one thing to review
ethical and legal principles in the abstract and quite another to rely
on them to make decisions when actual situations arise. The appropriate course of conduct and decision-making is governed by a variety of influences, including legal principles and ethics codes. Samuel
Knapp and Leon VandeCreek (2003), in introducing their book on
the 2002 revision of the American Psychological Association's
Ethics Code, state: 'Ethics Codes of professions are, by their very
nature, incomplete moral codes' (p. 7). Drawing on the information
covered so far in this book, the aim of this chapter is to move from
the abstract to the concrete, and in so doing model decision-making
processes for mental health professionals to assist them in dealing
with issues pertaining to confidentiality. To achieve this aim, two situations are identified in which mental health professionals face ethical dilemmas in relation to client or patient confidentiality.

The first situation pertains to a request for a psychiatrist to
release information about a patient to the patient's employer. In the
second case, the clinician wrestles with issues pertaining to the
patient's risk of harm to third parties. Once the cases have been presented, information is provided to work through the dilemmas using
a model for ethical decision-making presented in Figure 7.1. It is
hoped that these exercises will assist mental health professionals to

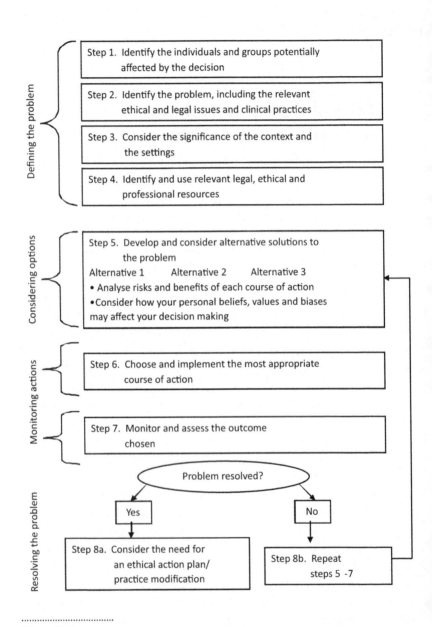

Figure 7.1
Decision-making model for resolving ethical dilemmas.

incorporate a systematic decision-making framework in their consideration of confidentiality-related ethical dilemmas. The exercises will also provide a good opportunity to learn how the principles that have been discussed throughout this book apply to actual dilemmas.

It is necessary to note a few general matters before proceeding. First, by their very nature, ethical dilemmas may not always have a single 'correct' outcome. Rather, some number of alternatives will inevitably arise to address such matters. Each alternative will have strengths and weaknesses. It is incumbent upon mental health professionals, therefore, to explore the options available and to evaluate the consequences and implications of each one before deciding how to proceed.

While it is possible that the decision reached by the mental health professional ends up being the 'wrong' decision, it is far worse, legally and professionally, to be negligent by not having gone through a careful decision-making process before arriving at a decision.

Second, as has been the case throughout this book, the challenge exists to state both principles that cover the law and ethical principles relevant to the different mental health professionals across different circumstances. As always, it is incumbent upon mental health professionals to be familiar with the code of ethics and their underlying values and principles governing their professions when considering ethical matters. Moreover, it is helpful for mental health professionals to have a working understanding of the relevant legal principles pertaining to confidentiality to guide their practices. The previous chapters have set out the relevant ethical and legal principles. As always, though, the information provided in considering the ethical dilemmas in this chapter is general in nature.

Third, it is important and helpful to seek professional advice from colleagues, superiors, professional bodies, indemnity insurers and legal counsel to assist in decision-making. Of course, time permitting, the more serious the situation, the longer the consultation should be. It is also prudent to document the information and advice received.

This chapter commences with the description of a decision-making model to establish a framework to help guide mental health professionals' decision-making. Scenarios will then be presented for consideration by readers. For each of the scenarios, the decision-making model and the information covered in this book will be applied to demonstrate how one may arrive at a decision in each matter.

A Model for Ethical Decision-Making

Mental health professionals, who may be highly skilled and knowledgeable in their fields, often approach matters that require ethical decision-making in an unsystematic and unsophisticated manner. Very often, by using a systematic model of decision-making, the most appropriate resolution of ethical dilemmas becomes apparent. In reviewing a number of different ethical decision-making models for mental health professionals, Samuel Knapp and Leon VandeCreek (2003) identify five steps shared by the various approaches:

- identification of the problem;
- development of alternatives;
- evaluation of alternatives;
- implementation of the best option; and
- evaluation of the results.

In addition to these steps, Knapp and VandeCreek propose that additional steps or factors are required to deal with emotional and situational factors, and point to the need for an immediate response in emergency situations. With respect to decision-making in emergency situations, the authors wisely suggest that mental health professionals should anticipate the sorts of ethical situations that may arise and develop ethical action plans to implement should the need arise. Without such already-established plans it may be too late or difficult to reasonably consider alternatives prior to needing to act in an emergency situation.

A useful model for decision-making that will be employed in this chapter is based on the model developed by Shane Bush, Mary Connell and Robert Denny (2006) as well as the work of the Canadian Psychological Association (2001). Drawing on the work of Knapp and VandeCreek (2003), Bush, Connell and Denny incorporate the five general steps noted above into their model. In addition, they outline the following three steps:

- consider the significance of the context and setting;
- identify and use ethical and legal resources; and
- consider personal beliefs and values.

The Canadian Psychological Association (2001) adds that the individuals and groups potentially affected by the decision should be identified and that the problem should be construed in accordance with the relevant ethical issues and practices being considered. Incorporating all of these steps, the model to be used in this chapter is presented in Figure 7.1. The steps will be defined as the example cases are resolved.

Sample Case Scenarios

In this section, two sample cases are presented. More detail will be provided as we work through the first case since this provides the first opportunity for practical application of the information pertaining to confidentiality reviewed throughout this book. Less detail will be required in the second case since the overarching principles will have been addressed in greater detail in the initial case.

For both case scenarios, Figure 7.1 should be referred to in order to see how the decision-making model and the questions posed throughout it are employed to guide the decision-making process. The aim of these exercises is to help you apply the information from this book in order to resolve actual dilemmas that may arise in your own practice.

Case 1: Requests for Obtaining Confidential Client Information

When Belinda was 17 years old she was admitted to the local Child and Adolescent Mental Health Service. Her parents reported that she was acting strangely, believing things that were not true. She was paranoid, became estranged from her friends and was reclusive. Upon examination, she was diagnosed with a psychotic illness not otherwise specified. Over time, the psychiatrist who treated her, Dr Waters, believed she had experienced the first episode of a schizophrenic illness. Belinda was in hospital for three weeks. Her symptoms stabilised and she was able to return home. She continued to see the mental health service on an outpatient basis. In the intervening two years, Belinda was hospitalised on three occasions. From the time she was 19 years old until she was 23, she had no further periods of hospitalisation, but was treated by Dr Waters on an out-patient basis.

Belinda was well enough to work and she obtained employment as a clerk in a department store. Things went well for her for several months and she was promoted to a supervisory position. Soon after, she began to deteriorate. She was once again paranoid and was unable to go to work. When she missed work, she obtained a medical certificate from Dr Waters, indicating she was unwell. As is the usual case, Dr Waters did not write the nature of Belinda's illness on the note; however, the letterhead on which the note was written indicated that Dr Waters was a psychiatrist.

When Belinda returned to work, the human resources manager asked to see her. Given that Belinda had acted strangely at work before she took time off, the human resources manager wanted to ensure she was fit to work. Belinda assured her that she was but declined to discuss the nature of her illness. She returned to work.

From the medical certificate Belinda provided, the human resources manager knew that she had been in the care of a psychiatrist. To allay her concerns, the manager telephoned Dr Waters, having obtained the telephone number from the certificate. The human resources manager told Dr Waters that Belinda worked for the store and that she was concerned about her capacity for work. The manager stated further that if she could not confirm that Belinda was fit to work, the store would be forced to let her go. Dr Waters wanted to be supportive of Belinda to help her keep her job.

How should the psychiatrist proceed?

Drawing on the decision-making model outlined in Figure 7.1, Case 1 will be analysed and resolved below.

Defining the Problem

The first four steps of the decision-making model provide an opportunity for the clinician to carefully define the nature and scope of the problem, as well as identify the resources necessary and available to assist them in resolving the dilemma. Each of these steps will be reviewed in turn.

Step 1: Identify the Individuals and Groups Potentially Affected by the Decision

In this dilemma, first and foremost Belinda, as the traditional patient or client, will be affected by Dr Waters' decision. Second, Belinda's employer may be affected by the decision. Third, Dr Waters will of course be affected by the decision and what she decides could affect the therapist–patient relationship she has with Belinda. Finally, although it is not specified in the scenario description, other individuals such as Belinda's family members or dependents may be affected by Dr Waters' decision.

Step 2: Identify the Problem, Including the Relevant Ethical and Legal Issues and Clinical Practices

Given that this book focuses on confidentiality, it almost goes without saying that confidentiality is the central ethical and legal issue in this and all of the other scenarios. Specifically, though, the ethical issue is whether Dr Waters should share information regarding her opinion of Belinda's capacity to work with the human resources manager. The legal issue is whether the information Dr Waters has regarding Belinda's health is protected under the state privacy legislation and, if so, whether and under what circumstances the information may be shared with the manager.

Step 3: Consider the Significance of the Context and the Settings

The situation is one in which the human resources manager is requesting information that is not consistent with the purpose for which it was initially collected — that is, for the health care of Belinda. The context in which the manager is seeking the information is highly unusual. To the extent that the employment is important to Belinda, however, the situation is significant. It is also worth noting that this situation is not an emergency.

Step 4: Identify and Use Relevant Legal, Ethical and Professional Resources

Dr Waters has a number of resources at her disposal:
- the relevant ethics code provisions:
  - 'Psychiatrists shall hold clinical information in confidence' (The RANZCP *Code of Ethics*, Principle 4);

- 'Confidentiality cannot always be absolute. A careful balance must be maintained between preserving confidentiality and the need to breach it rarely in order to promote the patient's best interests and/or safety and welfare of other persons' (The RANZCP *Code of Ethics*, Principle 4.5).
- the relevant Privacy Act and any other related Acts (e.g., *Health Records Act*) in her state;
- she can raise the matter with colleagues for advice;
- she can contact her medical indemnity insurer for legal advice; and
- she can consult a lawyer.

For the purposes of these exercises, it is assumed that in the information gathering phase, mental health professionals will have had an opportunity to explore their options for action with the various people noted above, and that they will have relied on the other resources as well.

Considering Options
Step 5: Develop and Consider Alternative Solutions to the Problem
Step 5 requires the clinician to begin to consider the alternative solutions to the dilemma. In demonstrating this process, we will review the relevant principles as we discuss the possible courses of action that Dr Waters may choose to follow.

Alternative 1: Do Not Disclose the Information
The general rule in considering matters pertaining to confidentiality is that the information obtained in the course of a clinical service is confidential. As such, the clinician must not share information about the patient or client, or even acknowledge that the individual is or has been their patient or client. As the ethical principles quoted above make clear, however, 'confidentiality cannot always be absolute'. Thus Dr Waters will need to determine whether Belinda's situation is such that an exception to the general rule might apply.

The usual circumstances in which confidential health care information may be shared occur when the purpose for sharing the information is consistent with the reason the information was initially obtained. In Belinda's situation, she has obtained psychiatric care from Dr Waters to treat her psychiatric illness. Given that the request by the human resources manager to obtain information about Belinda's care is to satisfy employment demands, the request is not consistent with the original purpose for which the information was obtained. Using this rationale, the first alternative is for Dr Waters to refuse to share the information with the human resources manager. Moreover, since the clinical relationship between Dr Waters and Belinda is confidential, Dr Waters may decide not to even acknowledge that Belinda is her patient.

Based on this alternative, Dr Waters may respond to the human resources manager: 'I am not in a position to even confirm that the person you are asking about is a patient of mine and certainly I would be unable to disclose *any* information to you about her, even if she was a patient of mine.'

Analyse risks and benefits of this course of action. The risk of this course of action is that Belinda may end up losing her employment because the human resources manager has not been assured that Belinda is fit to work. The benefit, however, is that Dr Waters will have protected Belinda's privacy by not revealing any information about the therapeutic relationship or any health information about Belinda. Moreover, by Dr Waters holding Belinda's information in confidence, she will ensure that Belinda trusts her, which will in turn protect the therapeutic relationship.

Consider how your personal beliefs, values and biases may affect your decision-making. In this scenario, Dr Waters has been providing psychiatric care to Belinda for several years; therefore, she will doubtless want to help Belinda. As such, it may be tempting to engage in a dialogue with the human resources manager to help protect Belinda by saving her job. Thus it will be tempting to share relevant information in a way that would serve to help Belinda maintain employment.

Alternative 2: Share the Information
While the first alternative may initially seem to be the only 'correct' course of action, the matter is perhaps more complicated than it first

appears. Indeed, the language from the ethical principles for psychiatrists is somewhat broad, providing that 'A careful balance must be maintained between preserving confidentiality and the need to breach it rarely in order to promote the patient's best interests and/or safety and welfare of other persons' (*The RANZCP Code of Ethics*, Principle 4.5). Dr Waters may need to ask whether it is in the 'best interests' of Belinda or other persons that she lose her job.

Further, it may be argued that Belinda waived her right to complete confidentiality when she requested that Dr Walters prepare the medical certificate that she submitted to her employer (that is, she implicitly consented to share information indicating that she was unwell and being treated by a psychiatrist). This is particularly the case since the letterhead indicated that Dr Waters is a psychiatrist. However, the information in the letter was limited in scope so that the extent to which the confidential information was shared was also limited.

Dr Waters is concerned that Belinda may lose her job, which has been an important part of her recovery. She realises that the human resources manager was calling to follow-up the medical certificate she completed. In this alternative, if she believes that it is in Belinda's best interests not to lose her job, Dr Waters may elect to provide information to the human resources manager to assure her that Belinda is fit for work. A complication would occur, of course, if Dr Waters does not believe that Belinda is fit for work and that the work would detrimentally affect her psychiatric wellbeing.

Analyse risks and benefits of this course of action. The risk with this course of action is that by electing to communicate with the human resources manager about Belinda, Dr Waters has violated Belinda's confidentiality. The benefit with this alternative is that Dr Waters believes she is protecting Belinda's employment.

Consider how your personal beliefs, values and biases may affect your decision-making. Dr Waters' beliefs and values will influence her decision-making. It is apparent that she is balancing her obligation to protect Belinda's privacy and the confidentiality of her treatment against the need to assure the human resources manager that Belinda is able to work, despite her illness.

Alternative 3: Compromise by Deferring the Decision to Belinda

Drawing on the need to balance two or more competing interests, which is typical in resolving ethical dilemmas, Dr Waters may contemplate a third alternative, one that offers a compromise to the first two courses of actions discussed. For this alternative, Dr Waters realises that she owes a duty of confidentiality to Belinda and that to share any information with the human resources manager may be seen as a violation of that duty. Although she did prepare the medical certificate, at Belinda's request, Dr Waters took care not to state the nature of the illness. From the letterhead the human resources manager discovered that Belinda was being treated by a psychiatrist, but that was the limit of the confidential information that was shared to that point.

The human resources manager clearly has concerns about Belinda's fitness to return to work. Therefore, Dr Waters may decide that since Belinda essentially holds the right of confidentiality, it must be her decision whether to allow Dr Waters to share any information with the manager. The extent to which patients value confidentiality varies, and it likely varies across situations as well. For example, while people may share confidential information with their friends, they may choose not to do so with their co-workers or employers. Therefore, it is always prudent, if possible, to check with patients to obtain an explicit indication of the value they place on confidentiality in particular situations.

For this third alternative, Dr Waters may decide to let the human resources manager know that she is unable to discuss any information pertaining to Belinda without first contacting her to seek her consent. Dr Waters could then contact Belinda to let her know that the human resources manager has been in touch. Dr Waters could engage Belinda in a dialogue about what, if any, information should be shared with the manager. They could agree on the limitations of confidential information that would be shared. For example, they could agree that Dr Waters would not reveal that Belinda has been diagnosed with schizophrenia or how she is being treated. Assuming Dr Waters believes that Belinda is now fit for work, they could agree that Dr Waters simply inform the human resources manager that Belinda has been in her care but has now recovered and is able to work. They could also agree that Dr Waters could further inform the manager that she will continue to see Belinda to assist her in maintaining her wellbeing. Dr Waters could also suggest that the manager contact Belinda to discuss the matter directly with her.

It is the case with this alternative that should Belinda decide she does not consent to Dr Waters sharing any information about her, Dr Waters will have to respect her wishes and not provide any information to the human resources manager.

Analyse risks and benefits of this course of action. This course of action minimises the risk of Belinda losing her job since the human resources manager could be assured that she is fit for work. Similarly, this alternative reduces or eliminates the risk of Dr Waters violating Belinda's right to confidentiality by revealing confidential information to the human resources manager without her consent. The benefit of this course of action is, therefore, that Belinda is likely to maintain her employment, assuming the human resources manager is content with the information shared by Dr Waters, with the minimum disclosure of Belinda's confidential health care information. Moreover, given protections afforded under legislation to people with disabilities, including mental illnesses, it would be difficult for the employer to dismiss Belinda due to a mental illness, as long as she was able to satisfactorily carry out her employment duties.

Consider how your personal beliefs, values and biases may affect your decision-making. For this course of action, Dr Waters' feelings of obligation to her patient can be respected while still helping to achieve the goal of assisting Belinda to maintain her employment.

Step 6: Choose the Most Appropriate Outcome
Alternative 3 appears to be the most appropriate course of action, particularly where the psychiatrist believes that Belinda is fit for work. This alternative allows the psychiatrist to share a limited amount of information, as agreed to by Belinda, to help preserve Belinda's employment. As such, the confidential information Belinda does not want shared — including, perhaps, the nature of the illness and other personal details — is held in confidence. Yet, enough information is shared with the human resources manager to hopefully preserve Belinda's employment.

Monitoring
Step 7: Monitor and Assess the Outcome Chosen
Having decided to proceed with the third alternative described above, Dr Waters would need to begin to implement the plan. She would need to contact Belinda and explain the options available to her. Assuming Belinda would consent to Dr Waters sharing the limited information with the human resources manager, Dr Waters could then contact the manager. Dr Waters would need to monitor whether the limited information Belinda has agreed to share — that she has a mental illness for which she has been successfully treated, that Dr Waters believes she is fit for work and that Dr Waters will continue to treat and monitor her — would satisfy the human resources manager at this point. If not, Dr Waters will need to reconsider her decision.

Resolving the Problem
Assuming Belinda and the human resources manager are satisfied with the planned course of action, the ethical dilemma should be resolved satisfactorily.

Step 8a: Consider the Need for an Ethical Action Plan or Practice Modification
Dr Waters would need to consider that when patients request medical certificates or letters for employers, they should be informed of the possibility that the employer may then learn that they have been in the care of a psychiatrist. This would hold true for other mental health professionals as well. In many circumstances, the patient could then opt to ask a general practitioner to prepare the certificate, given that most often the general practitioner and specialist mental health professional will be in communication about the patient's situation. If the patient does not mind the employer learning that they have been cared for by a mental health professional, then the mental health professional should discuss with the patient the nature of information to be shared in the medical certificate or note.

Step 8b: Repeat Steps 5–7
Steps 5 to 7 would need to be revisited if in the course of implementing or monitoring the situation Dr Waters realised that the plan was unsuccessful or inappropriate.

Case 2: Divulging Confidential Information to Protect Third Parties

Sebastian was a voluntary patient at the local Community Mental Health Service where he was seen regularly by Dr Suresh, a clinical psychologist. Sebastian was 31 years old and had a history of psychiatric illness. He received a disability support pension and lived in supported accommodation. While Sebastian had a history of making threats and becoming enraged, the psychologist did not believe that he had ever assaulted anyone. Similarly, although he was uncertain, the psychologist did not believe that Sebastian had a criminal history. Sebastian had a history of self-harm, including an occasion 18 months ago when he was rescued by staff after cutting his wrists and overdosing on benzodiazepines.

Dr Suresh found that, over the past three months, Sebastian was finding it increasingly difficult to control his anger. In particular, he was making threats to harm others. While the threats were diffused, he had targeted a young man, Adam, who had been living in the same accommodation until two weeks ago.

On the most recent occasion that Dr Suresh saw Sebastian, he was guarded on interview and initially downplayed the level of anger and distress he was experiencing. He exhibited delusional thinking, believing that others had targeted him and were conspiring against him. This was consistent with his past history of symptoms while he was unwell, although Sebastian had not verbalised such thoughts for more than two years.

Consistent with previous paranoid thinking, Sebastian expressed the belief that some co-residents were 'spies', placed there to monitor him. Over time, he admitted that he felt as though he was 'at the end of his rope' and ready to give up. He felt he was destined to end his own life. Again, this was consistent with previous suicidal thinking evidenced by Sebastian. However, unlike previous occasions, Sebastian discussed a desire to 'take someone with him' this time. When Dr Suresh queried this thinking, Sebastian replied that 'they' had caused him so much pain, he wanted them to know how he felt when he was targeted. Initially Sebastian denied having any particular person in mind. When pressed, though, Sebastian named the young male co-resident Adam, whom he had previously targeted.

Dr Suresh employed the HCR-20 violence risk assessment measure (Webster, Douglas, Eaves, & Hart, 1997) to assist with determining

Sebastian's level of risk for engaging in violence. Based on the information available, Dr Suresh formed the belief that at the present time he posed a high risk of harm to others and, in particular, to the co-resident Sebastian named — Adam.

How should the psychologist proceed?

Defining the Problem

As discussed with Case 1, the decision-making model requires the clinician to carefully define the nature of the dilemma, including the significance and context of the situation. These initial steps also make mental health professionals evaluate the legal, ethical and professional resources available and required to resolve the dilemma.

Step 1: Identify the Individuals and Groups Potentially Affected by the Decision

Dr Suresh has an ongoing, voluntary, therapeutic relationship with Sebastian. As such, Sebastian will be clearly affected by Dr Suresh's decision. The former co-resident whom Sebastian has targeted may also be affected by Dr Suresh's decision. As always, the clinician, Dr Suresh, will be affected by the decision, particularly in light of his relationship with Sebastian.

Step 2: Identify the Problem, Including the Relevant Ethical and Legal Issues and Clinical Practices

Although the case pertains — broadly speaking — to confidentiality, the narrow ethical issue to be addressed in this scenario is whether Dr Suresh should use information held in confidence to try to 'protect' the third party, Adam. There is a related legal issue: could Dr Suresh and/or the mental health service for which he works be civilly liable should he decide to protect Sebastian's confidentiality and Sebastian attacks and injures Adam? Conversely, there is a risk that Sebastian might take legal action against Dr Suresh and the mental health service if Dr Suresh decides to violate his confidentiality, and Sebastian believes it was wrongfully done. However, if Dr Suresh warns Adam or takes any measures to control Sebastian, Sebastian might lose his trust in Dr Suresh and no longer talk with him about why he is experiencing anger and distress.

Step 3: Consider the Significance of the Context and the Settings

Given Dr Suresh's conclusion that 'at the present time he posed a high threat of harm to others and, in particular, to the co-resident Sebastian named — Adam', the situation is serious. Indeed, Sebastian may cause harm to Adam or to someone else. Of concern as well is that should Dr Suresh violate Sebastian's confidentiality, their therapeutic relationship may be irrevocably harmed. The context is that Sebastian has been deteriorating and has expressed suicidal and homicidal ideation. This is in light of Sebastian's ongoing psychiatric illness.

Step 4: Identify and Use Relevant Legal, Ethical and Professional Resources

In this situation, Dr Suresh may consider the following:

- the relevant Australian Psychological Society ethics code provisions, which are as follows:
  - 'Psychologists safeguard the confidentiality of information obtained during their provision of psychological services' (The APS Code of Ethics, Standard A.5.1)
  - 'Psychologists disclose confidential information obtained in the course of their provision of psychological services only under any one or more of the following circumstances ... (c) if there is an immediate and specified risk of harm to an identifiable person or persons that can be averted only by disclosing information' (The APS Code of Ethics, Standard A.5.2)
  - 'Psychologists inform clients at the outset of the professional relationship, and as regularly thereafter as is reasonably necessary, of the: (a) limits to confidentiality; and (b) foreseeable uses of the information generated in the course of the relationship' (The APS Code of Ethics, Standard A.5.3)
  - 'When a standard of this Code allows psychologists to disclose information obtained in the course of the provision of psychological services, they disclose only that information which is necessary to achieve the purpose of the disclosure, and then only to people required to have that information' (The APS Code of Ethics, Standard A.5.4)

- 'Psychologists ensure consent is informed by: ... (h) explaining confidentiality and limits to confidentiality' (The APS Code of Ethics, Standard A.3.3)
- the Privacy Act in his State
- raising the matter with colleagues for advice
- contacting his professional indemnity insurer
- consulting a lawyer, including the legal department representing the mental health service.

Once again, for the purposes of these exercises, it is assumed that Dr Suresh will have had an opportunity to explore his options for action with the various people noted above, and that he will have relied on the other resources as well.

Considering Options
Step 5: Develop and Consider Alternative Solutions to the Problem
Alternative 1: Do Not Disclose the Information

For the first alternative course of action, it is always useful to consider the effect of maintaining confidentiality. As indicated above, the general principle regarding confidentiality, as reflected in *The APS Code of Ethics*, is that *'(p)sychologists* safeguard the confidentiality of information obtained during their provision of *psychological services'* (Standard A.5.1). Adhering to this general rule, Dr Suresh might choose to continue treating Sebastian with the aim of helping him to manage his risk through treatment. Based on this alternative, Dr Suresh may wish to increase the frequency of his contact with Sebastian to help manage the risk.

Analyse risks and benefits of this course of action. The risk of this course of action, obviously, is that Sebastian may end up causing harm to someone, particularly Adam. Because Dr Suresh has recognised that Sebastian poses a 'high risk' of causing harm to others, he may feel professionally responsible for not doing more to protect others, and for ensuring that Sebastian does not detrimentally affect his own life by harming others. In addition, as pointed out in chapter 5, although there is no common law 'duty to protect' third parties in Australia, it is conceivable that given the right set of facts, a court could find that a therapist is liable for the harm that ensues as a result of the foreseeable actions of a psychiatric patient.

While it is possible that some risks might arise from Dr Suresh's decision to maintain confidentiality and to continue to treat Sebastian, some possible benefits might also unfold. In particular, Dr Suresh will be able to maintain a therapeutic relationship with Sebastian. This relationship, and the treatment that Dr Suresh could provide, might serve to reduce Sebastian's level of risk while helping to ensure a stable, long-term therapeutic relationship. Finally, Dr Suresh's decision to maintain confidentiality is consistent with *The APS Code of Ethics*, which does not require a psychologist to share confidential information to protect third parties, but allows them to do so.

Consider how your personal beliefs, values and biases may affect your decision-making. Dr Suresh will doubtless have a desire to preserve the therapeutic relationship with Sebastian. However, in trying to preserve the relationship, he may be overly confident in his ability to monitor Sebastian and prevent him from causing harm to a third party. Thus, Dr Suresh will need to keep an open mind about the likelihood that he will be able to provide adequate treatment and monitoring to manage Sebastian's risk. Dr Suresh will also need to consider his own attitudes towards the police and other relevant authorities in deciding how to proceed.

Alternative 2: Share the Information to Protect Third Parties

Dr Suresh could consider taking steps beyond ongoing treatment to reduce Sebastian's risk of harming Adam, or other people. To accomplish this, he may consider breaching information held in confidence to try to contain the level of risk that he believes Sebastian presents, thereby protecting Adam. To this end, Dr Suresh may elect to contact the police or other authorities to share his concern that Sebastian may harm others. In addition, he may decide to try to contact Adam to let him know that he may be targeted by Sebastian for harm.

When deciding to undertake this course of action, Dr Suresh would need to consider whether he is in fact violating Sebastian's confidentiality. For example, *The APS Code of Ethics*, Standard

A.3.3, requires that '*(p)sychologists* ensure consent is informed by: ... (h) explaining confidentiality and limits to confidentiality'. Moreover, *The* APS *Code of Ethics,* Standard A.5.3, provides that '*(p)sychologists* inform *clients* at the outset of the *professional relationship*, and as regularly thereafter as is reasonably necessary, of the: (a) limits to confidentiality; and (b) foreseeable uses of the information generated in the course of the relationship'.

In accordance with these standards, if Dr Suresh informed Sebastian as part of the initial informed consent process that he may need to share confidential information should Sebastian present a risk of harm to identified third parties, then electing to share the information to protect the third party will not be seen as an improper breach of confidentiality. This is particularly true if Dr Suresh reiterated the fact that the information discussed may not be held in confidence once Dr Suresh commenced evaluating Sebastian for the purpose of the risk assessment.

Specifically, *The APS Code of Ethics,* Standard A.5.2, considers the grounds upon which information may be disclosed by psychologists as follows:

> (p)sychologists disclose confidential information
> obtained in the course of their provision of
> psychological services only under any one or more
> of the following circumstances ... (c) if there is an
> immediate and specified risk of harm to an identifi-
> able person or persons that can be averted only
> by disclosing information.

Thus, to disclose the confidential information to the police and/or to Adam (if Dr Suresh can contact him) requires Dr Suresh to be satisfied that not only is there a high risk of harm, but that the harm is 'imminent', the third party to be protected is identified and the risk of harm can only be averted by the psychologist disclosing the information.

Finally, once the psychologist makes a decision to share the confidential information, the psychologist must 'disclose only that information which is necessary to achieve the purpose of the disclosure, and then only to people required to have that information' (*The APS Code of Ethics,* Standard A.5.4). As such, Dr Suresh might inform the police of something similar to the following:

> I am a psychologist employed by X service. I have a patient, Sebastian [surname], whose behaviours have been escalating and I believe he presents a high risk of harming an identifiable person (Adam [surname]). He has a mental illness that is contributing to this condition. As a result, it is my opinion that he may harm someone, most likely Adam, whom he has targeted.

In addition to the above, the psychologist could share details about the patient's address, but must not share information about the particular nature of Sebastian's mental illness or any other information obtained in confidence that is not relevant for the police to assist with Dr Suresh's request to help protect Adam.

Analyse risks and benefits of this course of action. There are a number of risks associated with this course of action. First, it is questionable what the police would be able to achieve. While they do have powers under all of the state and territory mental health Acts to apprehend people who they believe are mentally ill and require treatment to protect them from harming themselves or others, police have few other options for how to proceed in cases where people are making vague threats to harm others. Second, Sebastian may become angry with Dr Suresh and refuse to continue to see him therapeutically. Similarly, Sebastian's trust in mental health professionals, generally, may be affected. Third, although Dr Suresh has judged Sebastian as being a high risk of harming others, that does not mean Sebastian will actually end up harming anyone. Thus, the therapeutic relationship — and Sebastian's confidence in mental health professionals — may be jeopardised unnecessarily. Finally, should Dr Suresh decide to share some of the confidential information pertaining to Sebastian, Sebastian may make a complaint, or take legal action, against Dr Suresh for breach of confidentiality.

The benefit of this action is that Dr Suresh may be able to help Sebastian contain his level of risk by having the police become involved. This, in turn, may help to protect Adam, assuming Sebastian would have engaged in violent or threatening behaviour against him. Moreover, this course of action would be in accordance with Dr Suresh's ethical obligations.

Consider how your personal beliefs, values and biases may affect your decision-making. Dr Suresh will need to monitor his own beliefs, values and biases to help ensure that his decision to disclose confidential information is made independent of his own biases. For example, he will need to consider whether his decision to share the confidential information is based on any of his own biases. For example, is he afraid of Sebastian, or does he mistakenly believe that mentally ill people are always violent?

Alternative 3: Compromise to Help Manage Sebastian's Level of Risk

For this alternative, Dr Suresh may consider a situation where he chooses to arrange for an involuntary hospital admission for Sebastian. In this scenario, Dr Suresh may elect to share confidential information about Sebastian in order to help arrange a period of involuntary hospitalisation. To this end, Sebastian may draw upon a psychiatrist member of his team to arrange for an involuntary hospitalisation. Dr Suresh will need to share enough information with the treating psychiatrist to assist him or her with making a determination about whether Sebastian might meet the criteria for involuntarily hospitalisation.

The mental health Acts across the states require that a medical practitioner (and sometimes other health practitioners) needs to examine the individual to determine whether, in their professional opinion, the patient suffers from a mental illness, presents a risk of harm to himself or herself or others, or is unable to care for himself or herself or will deteriorate significantly without the involuntary treatment.

As with the second alternative, Dr Suresh's actions as described here would not contradict his ethical obligations if he ensures that the risk is imminent, the victim is identifiable and the risk cannot be averted by some other means that would not necessitate breaking confidentiality. He would also need to ensure that the only information revealed is that which is necessary to assist the psychiatrist with obtaining the information necessary to conduct an assessment of the patient's suitability for involuntary hospitalisation.

Analyse risks and benefits of this course of action. There are two general risks associated with this proposed course of action. First, it may not ultimately serve to protect third parties from Sebastian since he may not be found eligible for involuntary hospitalisation (although this is unlikely given the facts, Sebastian's history of psychiatric illness and Sebastian's current symptoms). Second, Sebastian may take offence with Dr Suresh's decision to share confidential information with others in order to protect possible third parties. The benefits of this action are that Sebastian may in fact be hospitalised or treated on a community-based order that assists him to restore his mental well-being over time, thereby also reducing the level of risk he poses to third parties including Adam. The related benefit is that while Dr Suresh is sharing some information obtained in confidence, the information is being shared to assist Sebastian in his care — not to warn the police in order to somehow protect third parties including Adam. Also, the information Dr Suresh is sharing is shared with a psychiatrist who is also obliged to maintain confidentiality.

Consider how your personal beliefs, values and biases may affect your decision-making. Considerations in this section are similar to those discussed for the previous two alternatives. For this alternative, Dr Suresh will have to consider his own views regarding involuntary treatment. Some people have misgivings about compelling treatment, which is typically forced medication. Dr Suresh would have to consider the extent to which any such views are balanced against the need to reduce the likelihood that Sebastian may harm Adam, or some other person.

Step 6: Choose the Most Appropriate Outcome
On balance, the first alternative, to maintain confidentiality and to try to reduce Sebastian's risk by continued treatment, is unlikely to be suitable given Dr Suresh's own conclusion that Sebastian poses a high risk of harm to others, particularly Adam. Dr Suresh's ability to treat Adam satisfactorily given the description of his presentation and mental state is tenuous at best.

While the first alternative course of action discussed may not be sufficient to avert harm, the second course of action may be too extreme under the circumstances. Given Sebastian's history and mental state, particularly in light of his current behaviour and disordered thinking, he would likely meet the criteria for involuntarily hospitalisation. As such, contacting the police or informing the intended victim, Adam, of the pending risk would not be seen to be the only means by which the 'immediate and specified risk of harm' to Adam could be 'averted'. Indeed, Sebastian is a known patient to the mental health service where Dr Suresh works. Dr Suresh would have ready access to psychiatrists or other suitable medical practitioners such as registrars or advanced trainees who can assist with a determination of whether involuntary hospitalisation or at least a community-based order is appropriate. Of course, if involuntary hospitalisation is not possible, or Sebastian's risk of harm to Adam could not be contained and eventually reduced through involuntary treatment and/or hospitalisation, Alternative 2 may become necessary.

Based on the considerations above, the third course of action would appear to satisfy Dr Suresh's need to reduce Sebastian's level of risk to protect Adam, while still preserving most of the confidential information revealed in the therapeutic relationship. Moreover, the purpose for which the confidential information was obtained through the therapeutic relationship — that is, to assist Sebastian with his mental and psychological wellbeing — is quite consistent with the ongoing provision of mental health treatment to Sebastian, albeit involuntary.

Monitoring
Step 7: Monitor and Assess the Outcome Chosen
Monitoring would be necessary and helpful in this situation to ensure that Sebastian's level of risk is being managed and that, whichever alternative course of action is in place, Adam is not likely to be harmed.

Resolving the Problem
If Sebastian's level of risk is managed and reduced without him causing harm to Adam, or other third parties, then the immediate problem will be resolved. If not, the information below will need to be considered to modify the plan of action.

Step 8a: Consider the Need for an Ethical Action Plan or Practice Modification

First, there is a need to ensure that Sebastian's level of risk is being managed and hopefully reducing. Second, should it be found that Sebastian does not satisfy the requirements for involuntary hospitalisation or treatment, Alternative 2 would need to be reconsidered and likely adopted. Third, even with treatment, Sebastian's level of risk to Adam may not reduce sufficiently prior to discharge, thereby necessitating the consideration of following the second alternative.

Step 8b: Repeat Steps 5–7

Steps 5 to 7 would need to be reconsidered if in the course of monitoring the situation it was found that the plan was not successful or appropriate.

Conclusions

As suggested by the information presented in this chapter, employing a comprehensive decision-making model to assist with considering ethical dilemmas provides a useful mechanism for mental health professionals to decide how to act on a case-by-case basis. Furthermore, as the two exercises revealed, the process of considering and resolving ethical dilemmas regarding confidentiality is fluid and complex. The mental health professional needs to consider the various ethical and legal principles in order to arrive at an appropriate and effective resolution.

While it may not always be clear exactly which alternative course of action will be 'correct' under the circumstances, the structured decision-making process ensures adequate consideration of the factors that mental health professionals must consider prior to making a decision on how to proceed in the most appropriate manner. Ongoing monitoring is then required, along with modification of the plan or implementation of alternative courses of action as necessary.

CHAPTER 8

Quick Guides

The previous chapters introduced a basic understanding of the ethical and legal principles relating to confidentiality in therapeutic settings. As most of the relevant principles leave much scope for interpretation, this book aims to provide guidance for mental health professionals as to how to understand the underlying reasons why ethics and the law protect confidentiality. The book's main aim is to assist in the appropriate application of the relevant principles and avoidance of unnecessary breaches of confidentiality.

This book suggests that mental health professionals should not adopt an over-cautious approach to disclosing confidential information. While many mental health professionals may be concerned about being sued by clients or patients if they disclose certain information, it is important to recognise that a duty to maintain confidentiality cannot be absolute.

The common law has identified a range of situations in which mental health professionals have discretion as to whether or not to disclose confidential information. In Australia, the common law has *not* established a duty to warn third parties about clients or patients considered at risk of harming others. Indeed, the courts in England, New Zealand and Australia have been hesitant to impose such a duty. The few instances in which mental health professionals *must* disclose certain confidential information, such as information regarding child abuse, are provided for in specific legislation.

This approach indicates that the law does recognise that a dilemma exists for mental health professionals when faced with the difficult task of having to make a decision in a time of crisis where the choice seems to be one of two wrong actions: to breach confidentiality or to take the risk, even a most remote risk, of a worst-case scenario coming true.

Ethics and the law recognise that the question whether confidential information may or should be disclosed is a matter of reasonably balancing the interests at stake and the options at hand. The actual process of decision-making is central to establishing whether a mental health professional has acted appropriately. The suggested decision-making model set out in chapter 7 for resolving ethical dilemmas serves to guide mental health professionals as to how to make a decision that is well-balanced and appropriate. The decision-making process should be guided by an individual assessment of the problem and the options available, and a realistic consideration of what can be done to minimise any possible harm.

Ethical considerations are relevant for the interpretation and application of the law. The law on confidentiality relies on terminology that is open to interpretation, such as what is 'reasonable' or what is 'appropriate'. Where these kinds of terms are included in legal provisions, the law can be guided by ethics, as ethics reflect universally applicable values and principles. These kinds of values and principles aid the development of the common law, and many statutes recognise general principles in their introductory statements on the purpose, objects or functions of the particular Act. Mental health legislation is, for example, typically based on the guiding objective to provide the best possible and least restrictive outcome for the client or patient. It can, for example, clarify that its objects are to facilitate the treatment of clients or patients or to protect the rights of people with mental illnesses.

Human rights–based arguments that are founded on general ethical principles are increasingly being used in the interpretation of Australian law. A general knowledge of the fundamentals of ethics is therefore helpful in situations where the law is open to interpretation. An understanding of ethical principles can also provide mental health professionals with a systematic framework to help clarify what criteria should be considered in order to reach a well-considered and well-reasoned decision.

The decision-making model for resolving ethical dilemmas set out in chapter 7 sets out what needs to be taken into account in order to reach a high standard of decision-making. While the decision-making model for resolving ethical dilemmas is central to this book, this chapter aims to bring together some of the central features of the previous chapters. These features are summarised in the following overview. It includes some of the central considerations on confidentiality in current law and ethics and provides a quick reference to criteria that can be used in conjunction with the decision-making model for resolving ethical dilemmas.

A Quick Guide to Ethical Principles

- There is a variety of different theories of ethics that all hold that confidentiality is fundamentally important in therapeutic relationships.
- Maintaining confidentiality serves to uphold the following principles:
  - not to cause harm to the client or patient;
  - to benefit the client or patient;
  - to respect the client's or patient's autonomy; and
  - to serve justice.
- Confidentiality is also interrelated to respecting a person's right to autonomy, a right which is of fundamental importance in health settings.
- While it is important to respect and maintain confidentiality wherever possible, on occasion it may be ethical to disclose confidential information.
- When faced with a choice between 'morally right' options, a solution can be based on the decision-making model for resolving ethical dilemmas set out in chapter 7.

A Quick Guide to Legal Principles

- The common law and international human rights law generally protects confidentiality in therapeutic relationships.
- The common law emphasises that disclosure of confidential information should be exceptional in nature.

- In weighing up whether to disclose confidential information on the basis of risk of harm, the courts have looked at whether:
  - there is a clear risk to an identifiable person or group of persons;
  - there is an imminent risk of serious bodily or psychological harm or death; and
  - the public interest protected by the duty of confidence is outweighed by the public interest in minimising the risk of harm.
- Australian courts have not established a 'duty to protect' or a 'duty to warn' third parties and it seems unlikely that such a duty will be imposed.
- Australian courts have permitted the disclosure of confidential information in certain circumstances.
- Some of the most important statutory provisions dealing with confidentiality can be found in privacy and health records legislation, mental health Acts, and legislation dealing with the mandatory disclosure of information regarding child abuse.
- Australian legislation mandates breaching confidentiality only in limited, clearly identified situations, such as the mandatory reporting of child abuse.

A Quick Guide to Respecting Confidentiality in Practice

- Familiarise yourself with your profession's current code of ethics in general, and its specific provisions on confidentiality.
- Be aware that it is your ethical and professional responsibility to respect your client's or your patient's rights, not just his or her right to have confidentiality respected. In this context:
  - Do not disclose confidential information, if the disclosure may identify your client or patient.
  - Do not use confidential information for purposes outside the therapeutic relationship.
  - Protect your records, communication and disposal of confidential information.

- Talk with your client or patient about confidentiality at the outset of the therapeutic relationship and subsequently as often as you consider it reasonably necessary to clarify your client's or patient's expectations. In this regard:
  - Explain that you will maintain and respect confidentiality wherever possible, but that there may be limits to guaranteeing confidentiality.
  - Outline some of the specific circumstances where disclosure of confidential information may be made.
  - Tailor the initial discussion of confidentiality to the kind of service you provide, the expectations of your client or patient in the light of his or her social and cultural background, and your practical experience.
- If you decide that you will disclose confidential information, try to approach your client or patient first with the aim of gaining consent, unless this approach is unreasonable or inappropriate in the given circumstances.
- If you think there is a risk that your client may harm others, use the decision-making model for resolving ethical dilemmas suggested in chapter 7 and consider the following issues:
  - Is there a clear and imminent risk of serious bodily or psychological harm or death?
  - Will disclosing the information substantially reduce the risk?
  - Can approaching another health professional help you reach a decision?
  - Does the protection of the public outweigh the interests of the client or patient in preserving confidentiality?
  - Can the disclosure of confidential information be reduced to the minimum that is necessary to avoid the risk?

Conclusion

In chapter 1, it was noted that there is often confusion as to whether mental health professionals are obliged to disclose confidential information and, if so, what information they may have to disclose and to whom. It is hoped that this book has provided some clarification as to the legal and ethical principles relating to confidentiality, and provided guidance as to the decision-making process in deciding whether or not to disclose confidential information. If there are concerns about specific situations, it is important and helpful to seek professional advice from colleagues, superiors, professional bodies, indemnity insurers and legal counsel to assist in decision-making.

Table of Cases

Hunter v Mann [1974] QB 767, 37, 71
Hunter Area Health Service v Presland (2005) 63 NSWLR 22, 72, 73

Kadian v Richards (2004) 61 NSWLR 222, 37, 71–72
Kirkland-Veenstra v Stuart (2008) Aust Torts Reports ¶81–936, 72

Maulolo v Hutt Valley Health Corporation Ltd [2002] NZAR 375, 68

Parry-Jones v Law Society [1969] 1 Ch 1, 37, 38, 44
Presland v Hunter Area Health Service [2003] NSWSC 754, 72

R v Lowe [1997] 2 VR 465, 70–71
Richards v Kadian (2005) 64 NSWLR 204, 71
Rogers v Whitaker (1992) 175 CLR 479, 45–46, 52
Royal Women's Hospital v Medical Practitioners Board of Victoria (2006) 15 VR 22, 71

Smith v Jones (1999) 132 CCC (3d) 239, 62–63
Stevens v Avery [1988] 2 All ER 477, 55
Stuart v Kirkland-Veenstra (2009) 237 CLR 215, 72
Sullivan v Moody (2001) 207 CLR 562, 52

Tarasoff v Regents of the University of California 17 Cal 3d 425 (1976), 61–62, 67

Van de Wetering v Capital Coast Health Limited (unreported, High Court of New Zealand, Wellington Registry, 19 May 2000), 67–68

W v Edgell [1990] 1 All ER 835, 64–65
Wainwright v Home Office [2003] 3 WLR 1337, 55

Table of Statutes

Northern Territory
Care and Protection of Children Act 2007
  s 26, 88
Information Act 2006
  s 148, 78
Mental Health and Related Services Act 2005, 86
  s 91(2)(f)–(h), 85
  s 91(2)(g), 85

Queensland
Child Protection Act 1999
  s 22, 91
Civil Liability Act 2003, 47
  s 9, 49
Mental Health Act 2000
  s 528(1)–(2), 80
  s 528(3)(b), 80
  s 528(3)(c), 80
  s 528(3)(d), 80
  s 529(3)(a), 80
  s 529(3)(b), 80
  s 530, 80
Public Health Act 2005
  s 191, 88

South Australia
Children's Protection Act 2003
  s 11, 88
Civil Liability Act 1936
  s 32, 47
Mental Health Act 2009, 86
  s 106(1), 81
  s 106(2)(a), 81
  s 106(2)(b), 81
  s 106(2)(c), 81
  s 106(2)(e), 81, 85
  s 106(2)(f), 81

References

Australian Association of Occupational Therapists. (2001). *Code of ethics.* Melbourne, Australia: Author.

Australian Association of Social Workers. (2002). *Code of ethics.* Canberra, Australia: Author.

Australian Psychological Society. (2007). *Code of ethics.* Melbourne, Australia: Author.

Australian Psychological Society. (2008). *Ethical guidelines complementing the APS Code of Ethics.* Melbourne, Australia: Author.

Australian Psychological Society. (2005). *Guidelines for working with people who pose a high risk of harming others.* Melbourne, Australia: Author.

Australian Psychological Society. (2007). *Guidelines on confidentiality.* Melbourne, Australia: Author.

Beauchamp, T.L. (2007). The 'four principles' approach to health care ethics. In R.E. Ashcroft, A. Dawson, H. Draper & J. McMillan (Eds.), *Principles of health care ethics* (2nd ed., pp. 3–10). Chichester, UK: John Wiley and Sons.

Beauchamp, T.L. (2009). The philosophical basis of psychiatric ethics. In S. Bloch & S.A. Green (Eds.), *Psychiatric ethics* (4th ed., pp. 25–48). Oxford, UK: Oxford University Press.

Beauchamp, T., & Childress, J. (2001). *Principles of biomedical ethics* (5th ed). New York: Oxford University Press.

Bentham, J. (1793). *An introduction to the principles of morals and legislation.* Whitefish, MT: Kessinger Publishing (2005 reprint).

Bloch, S., & Green, S.A. (2006). An ethical framework for psychiatry. *British Journal of Psychiatry, 188*(1), 7–12.

Bloch, S., & Pargiter, R. (2009). Codes of ethics in psychiatry. In S. Bloch & S.A. Green (Eds.) *Psychiatric ethics* (4th ed., pp. 151–173). Oxford, UK: Oxford University Press.

Bush, S.S., Connell, M.A., & Denny, R.L. (2006). *Ethical practice in forensic psychology: A systematic model for decision making.* Washington, DC: American Psychological Association.

Canadian Psychological Association. (2001). *Companion manual to the Canadian code of ethics for psychologists* (3rd ed.). Ottawa, Canada: Author.

Crowden, A. (2003). Ethically sensitive mental health care: Is there a need for a unique ethics for psychiatry? *Australian and New Zealand Journal of Psychiatry*, *37*(2), 143–149.

Davidson, G. (1995). The ethics of confidentiality: Introduction. *Australian Psychologist, 30*(3), 153–157.

DeGrazia, D. (2003). Common morality, coherence, and the principles of biomedical ethics. *Kennedy Institute of Ethics Journal, 13*(3), 219–230.

Devereux, J. (2007). *Australian medical law* (3rd ed.). London & New York: Routledge-Cavendish Publishing.

Francis, R.D. (1999). *Ethics for psychologists: A handbook.* Camberwell, Victoria, Australia: Australian Council for Educational Research.

Freckelton, I. (2003). Liability of psychiatrists for failure to certify. *Psychiatry, Psychology and Law, 10*(2), 397–401.

Gillon, R. (1986). *Philosophical medical ethics.* Chichester, UK: John Wiley and Sons.

Gutheil, T.G. (2009). Ethics in forensic psychiatry. In S. Bloch & S.A. Green (Eds.), *Psychiatric ethics* (4th ed., pp. 151–173). Oxford, UK: Oxford University Press.

Hands, P. (1999). To disclose or not to disclose? Confidentiality and privilege. *Psychotherapy in Australia, 5*(2), 58–63.

Häyry, M. (2007). Utilitarianism and Bioethics. In R.E. Ashcroft, A. Dawson, H. Draper & J. McMillan (Eds.), *Principles of health care ethics* (2nd ed., pp. 57–64). Chichester, UK: John Wiley and Sons.

Herdy, W. (1996). Must the doctor tell? *Journal of Law and Medicine, 3*(3), 270–282.

Ipp, D. (2007). The politics, purpose and reform of the law of negligence. *Australian Law Journal, 81*(7), 456–464.

Ipp Committee Report, Panel of Eminent Persons to Review the Law of Negligence (the Ipp Committee). (2002). *Review of the law of negligence* (Final report). Canberra, Australia: Author.

Kämpf, A., & McSherry, B. (2006). Confidentiality in therapeutic relationships: The need to develop comprehensive guidelines for mental health professionals. *Psychiatry, Psychology and Law, 13*(1), 124–131.

Kämpf, A., McSherry, B., Thomas, S., & Abrahams, H. (2008). Psychologists' perceptions of legal and ethical requirements for breaching confidentiality. *Australian Psychologist, 43*(3), 194–204.

Kerridge, I., Lowe, M., & Stewart, C. (2009). *Ethics and law for the health professions* (3rd ed.). Sydney, Australia: Federation Press.

Knapp, S.J., & VandeCreek, L.D. (2003). *A guide to the 2002 revision of the American Psychological Association's ethics code.* Sarasota, FL: Professional Resource Press/Professional Resource Exchange.

Knapp, S.J., & VandeCreek, L.D. (2006). *Practical ethics for psychologists: A positive approach.* Washington, DC: American Psychological Association.

Knowles, A.D., & McMahon, M. (1995). Expectations and preferences regarding confidentiality in the psychologist–client relationship. *Australian Psychologist, 30*(3), 175–178.

Koocher, G.P. (1995). Confidentiality in psychological practice. *Australian Psychologist, 30*(3), 158–163.

Koocher, G.P., & Keith-Spiegel, P. (2008). *Ethics in psychology and the mental health professions: Standards and cases* (3rd ed.). New York: Oxford University Press.

Kottow, M. (1986). Medical confidentiality: An intransigent and absolute obligation. *Journal of Medical Ethics, 12*(3), 117–122.

Law Reform Commission. (1983). *Privacy Vol. 2 — Proposals* (Report No. 22). Canberra, Australia: Australian Government Publishing Service.

Manning, J. (2007). The standard of care and expert evidence of accepted practice in medical negligence. *Journal of Law and Medicine, 15*(3), 394–407.

McIlwraith, J., & Madden, B. (2006). *Health care and the law* (4th ed.). Sydney, Australia: Lawbook Co.

McMahon, M. (1992). Dangerousness, confidentiality, and the duty to protect. *Australian Psychologist, 27*(1), 12–16.

McMahon, M. (2006). Re-thinking confidentiality. In I. Freckelton & K. Peterson (Eds.), *Disputes and dilemmas in health law* (pp. 563–603). Sydney, Australia: The Federation Press.

McSherry, B. (2001). Confidentiality of psychiatric and psychological communications: The public interest exception. *Psychiatry, Psychology and Law, 8*(1), 12–22.

Mendelson, D., & Mendelson, G. (1991). Tarasoff Down Under: The psychiatrist's duty to warn in Australia. *Journal of Psychiatry and Law, 19*, 33–60.

Michalowski, S. (2003). *Medical confidentiality and crime.* Burlington, VT: Ashgate.

Mill, J.S. (1895). *On liberty.* Harmondsworth, UK: Penguin Classics Publishing.

Milne, J. (1995). An analysis of the law of confidentiality with special reference to the counselling of minors. *Australian Psychologist, 30*(3), 169–174.

Moore, G.E., & Baldwin, T. (1993). *Principia ethica* (2nd ed.). Cambridge, UK: Cambridge University Press.

Oakley, J., & Cocking, D. (2001). *Virtue ethics and professional roles.* Cambridge, UK: Cambridge University Press.

Office of the Privacy Commissioner. (2005). *Getting in on the Act: The review of the private sector provisions of the Privacy Act 1988.* Sydney, Australia: Australian Government Office of the Privacy Commissioner.

Pellegrino, E., & Thomasma, D. (1993). *The virtues in medical practice.* New York: Oxford University Press.

Radden, J. (2002). Notes towards a professional ethics for psychiatry. *Australian and New Zealand Journal of Psychiatry, 36*(1), 52–59.

Rangarajan, S., & McSherry, B. (2009). To detain or not to detain: A question of public duty? *Psychiatry, Psychology and Law, 16*(2), 288–302.

Royal Australian and New Zealand College of Psychiatrists. (2004). *The RANZCP Code of Ethics.* Melbourne, Australia: Author.

Scott, R. (2006). *Hunter Area Health Services v Presland:* Liability of mental health services for failing to admit or detain a patient with a mental illness. *Psychiatry, Psychology and Law, 13*(1), 49–59.

Singer, P. (1993). *Practical ethics* (2nd ed.). Cambridge, UK: Cambridge University Press.

Skene, L. (2008). *Law and medical practice: Rights, duties, claims and defences* (3rd ed.). Sydney, Australia: LexisNexis Butterworths.

Sperry, L. (2007). *The ethical and professional practice of counseling and psychotherapy.* Boston: MA: Pearson, Allyn and Bacon.

Travers, R. (2002). Medical causation. *Australian Law Journal, 76*(4), 258–268.

Walcott, D.M., Cerundolo, P., & Beck, J.C. (2001). Current analysis of the Tarasoff duty: An evolution towards the limitation of the duty to protect. *Behavioural Sciences and the Law, 19*, 325–343.

Webster, C.D., Douglas, K.S., Eaves, D., & Hart, S.D. (1997). *HCR-20: Assessing the risk for violence* (Version 2). Burnaby, Canada: Mental Health, Law and Policy Institute, Simon Fraser University.

Index

CPSIA information can be obtained
at www.ICGtesting.com
Printed in the USA
FSOW03n1954060415
6281FS

9 781921 513428